NUCLEAR-FREE DEFENCE

Edited by Louis Mackay and David Fernbach

NUCLEAR-FREE DEFENCE

A symposium with contributions by

Ronald Higgins	Stephen Maxwell	Pat Arrowsmith
Frank Allaun MP	John Shiers	Joan Maynard MP
Mary Kaldor	Stuart Christie	Meg Beresford
Bennie Bunsee	Ruth Wallsgrove	Robert Fyson
Lisa Foley	Dafydd Elis Thomas MP	Ann Pettit
David Widgery	David Selbourne	Chris Savory
April Carter	Carole Harwood	David Taylor
Peter Tatchell		Jonathan Moore

heretic books

First published in May 1983 by Heretic Books,
  P O Box 247, London N15 6RW, England

Introduction world copyright   ©1983 Heretic Books; contributions
  world copyright   ©1983 each author

Royalties from this book are being donated by agreement with
  the authors to peace-movement organisations

British Library Cataloguing in Publication Data
  Nuclear-free defence.
    1. Atomic warfare   2. Deterrence (Strategy)
    I. Mackay, Louis   II. Fernbach, David
    355'.0217   UF767

    ISBN 0 946097 04 6

The following contributors responded to the questionnaire orally
and subsequently corrected the transcripts made:
  Frank Allaun, Pat Arrowsmith, Mary Kaldor, Joan Maynard.

Cover by Louis Mackay
Photoset by Shanta Thawani, 25 Natal Road, London N11
Printed and bound by Book Plan (Billing & Sons) Ltd, Worcester

Contents

(The full text of the relevant question
is given at the start of each section)

Introduction

The Cold War is back. Since the later phase of the Carter administration, when the frost set in again, the world has become a more dangerous place. The arms race, which never stopped, has accelerated and new weapons of mass destruction are being developed and produced. Governments in both West and East, notwithstanding the severe economic and social problems they are facing, have increased their military budgets at the expense of other sectors of their economies. New strategic doctrines have come to the fore, emphasising the use of nuclear weapons in a 'fightable' war over their supposed deterrent role.

The mounting sense of insecurity on the East-West axis has been accompanied by a similar phenomenon on the North-South axis; poor countries, faced with the economic chaos of the deepening world recession and accumulating debts, have watched the rich countries seeking first to protect their own advantage. Long-standing conflicts in the Middle East, in eastern and southern Africa and in south-east Asia have continued unresolved while new wars in Afghanistan, on the border between Iran and Iraq, in Africa and in Latin America have created new zones of conflict. After decades during which membership of the Nuclear Weapons Club was restricted to the superpowers and Britain, France and China, there is now the prospect of several countries in, or close to, areas of conflict, including Israel, Iraq, Libya, India, Pakistan, South Africa, Brazil and Argentina, becoming nuclear weapons states in the near future — and some may already have done so without seeing any advantage in announcing it to the world. All this has brought the danger of nuclear war closer.

At the same time there is a growing public awareness of the danger. Peace movements have arisen — or been revived — in many countries and have reached unprecedented strength. And criticism of current military policies is by no means restricted to the radical fringe or to the organisations campaigning for unilateral nuclear disarmament. An unease concerning the direction of these policies — to say nothing of their expense — is affecting sections of all the major British political parties and even elements of the military. Field-Marshal Lord Carver, for instance, has been an outspoken critic both of Trident and of NATO's refusal to make a 'no first use' commitment regarding nuclear weapons. As a result, the question of defence policy is coming in for more public and more critical examination than at any time since the end of the Second World War.

In Britain the arguments over nuclear weapons have reached a wide public, thanks largely to the efforts of such organisations as the Campaign for Nuclear Disarmament, European Nuclear Disarmament and the World Disarmament Campaign. But while the case for nuclear disarmament has been understood by many people (though not yet enough) and while much has been said and written about the folly of current policies, less attention has been paid to the question of what sort of defence policies should be adopted to replace nuclear Atlanticism. One reason for this has been the general difficulty of debating defence matters in Britain, where such debate has been actively discouraged by the obsessive secrecy of British governments and where defence policy decisions are often not even discussed in Parliament, but only in the restricted circles of an elite of specialists supposed to have the information the public lack. James Callaghan's decision to authorise the £1,000 million 'Chevaline' programme was taken with the knowledge of only three other members of the Cabinet, in defiance of the Labour party's declared policy, and kept secret until the succeeding Conservative govern- ment chose to reveal it to Parliament. Similarly, that Conservative government's decision, in 1979, to accept the stationing of American cruise missiles in Britain in 1983 was made without reference to Parliament. Discussion of defence has also been inhibited by the fact that many of the basic assumptions that have underlain defence policy — including views of Britain's role in the world and the priority given to the relationship between Eastern and Western spheres of influence over the balance of power on the North-South axis — are deeply rooted and largely shared across the parliamentary political spectrum. Apart from this, there has been a reluctance on the Left to tackle the issues involved in anything but vague terms. This may stem in part from anti-militarism, in part from mixed attitudes towards the USSR and towards Europe, and in part from a tacit recognition of the difficulty of bringing about major changes in defence policy without at the same time achieving other major changes in society, in the economy and in international relations.

Recently the work of bodies such as the Alternative Defence Commission, based at the Bradford University School of Peace Studies, has done much to focus more attention on examining defence alternatives. We hope this book will help to make participation in this discussion still broader.

Criticism of military policy has a long history in association with radical movements. Pacifism, the refusal of all violence on the basis of philosophical or religious principles, has ancient origins and was preached by dissident sects under the Roman empire and by millenarian movements in the Middle Ages. But there have also been military critiques from other points of view. Since the time of Oliver Cromwell, radical proposals have included the establishment of a national army in place of corrupt professional armies, the introduction of general conscription, and the adoption of systems based on citizens' or workers' militias. After the carnage of 1914-18, 'the war to end war', pacifist movements flourished for a time before falling into relative disfavour during the Second World War, which many people saw as a just war. The advent of atomic weapons threw the whole question of fighting wars into a new context as it became clear that nuclear war threatened the survival not only of individuals, communities and nations but of the human species.

The existence of nuclear weapons has not however put an end to war in the world — in spite of the arguments of the nuclear apologists who credit their weapons for the relative peace of Europe during the last 38 years. The period since 1945 has, on the contrary, seen some of the most destructive wars in human history and many of them have involved a nuclear weapons state, directly or by proxy, on at least one side. Some of these wars have been seen as national liberation struggles — part of a necessary process of redistributing power in the world — and in the Vietnam war, for example, many people on the Left saw guerrilla tactics, political conviction and morale triumph over the massive destructive power and technology of the United States. There is an argument that suchǀguerrillaǀtactics,suitably adapted and advertised, could play an important part in a non-nuclear defence policy for a country such as Britain. Others look rather to the example of the non-violent resistance of Gandhi and his followers in the struggle to liberate India from British colonial domination, and advocate strictly non-violent forms of 'civilian defence' or 'social defence'.

The international peace movement today (and there is such a movement whose parts are conscious of the whole) is necessarily a loose, decentralised organism that takes different forms in different parts of the world. What is possible in one country may not be possible in another. This movement functions on a variety of international networks — through local peace groups, political and religious organisations, trade unions, associations of scientists, doctors and journalists, etc. It comprises unilateralists and multilateralists and others who see scope for both unilateral and multilateral action. It includes 'pragmatists' and 'idealists', pacifists and non-pacifists. A movement is not a static position; it is a shift in a certain direction, a river with many tributaries. Idealism and pragmatism are not antagonistic opposites but complementary components; one without the other is inadequate; together they create a potential. The peace movement would be poorer without the constructive tension that exists between its parts. Our hope, in presenting the various viewpoints contained in this book, is that they will each contribute in their own way to the general movement.

The speed and strength with which the movement for peace and nuclear disarmament has revived has astonished and alarmed its opponents. It has become a major political factor in many Western countries. In the USA, the 'freeze' movement has created serious difficulties for Reagan over getting the MX missile programme funded, and it looks as though nuclear weapons policy will play a central role in the next presidential election. All across Europe, from Iceland to Turkey (a NATO country in which peace activists, like other critics of the military regime, are being subjected to fierce repression), the nuclear weapons issue is threatening to upset political applecarts. In northern Europe especially — in Britain, Benelux, Denmark, Norway, and perhaps most importantly in West Germany (where it has been largely responsible for the emergence, in a position of considerable importance, of a new political element — the Greens), the issue has become one on which some of the major political parties may stand or fall. A Gallup poll conducted in Britain in October 1982 indicated that 56-58 per cent of the British population are opposed to Trident and cruise and this has given the Conservative government perhaps its biggest cause for worry since the Falklands war. The Labour party, sensing that *a measure* of nuclear disarmament could now be a vote-winner rather than a vote-loser, is making the cancellation of cruise and Trident a prominent feature in its programme. It remains to be seen what this would mean in the event of a Labour victory at the next general election.

It is not only in the West that the effect has been felt. Certainly, there is in the foreseeable future no possibility of a mass peace movement, on the pattern of those in the West, existing in the USSR — apart from the official organisations which are uncritical of Soviet policy (though even these, somewhere behind the closed doors which conceal the workings of state power, may not be as monolithically one-sided as they appear). The small, independent peace groups which exist in several cities in the USSR are struggling against harassment and KGB attempts to depict them as hooligans and lunatics. In the GDR and in Hungary, however, independent non-aligned peace groups have managed to create some room for themselves and to maintain a more or less open, if uneasy, relationship with the state authorities. These are certainly a cause for anxiety in Moscow.

The European peace movement has presented the Soviet Union with a conundrum. On the one hand, its effect on Western public opinion in a certain sense obviously works in favour of a sense of security in the USSR — to the extent that it serves to counter a military build-up in the West. And on this count it is in the Soviet interest to present the Western peace movements in a favourable light to the people of the Warsaw Pact countries. On the other hand, with the lid barely on Poland, the support the Western peace groups have expressed for Solidarność and Charter 77, and their condemnation of the Soviet invasion of Afghanistan, of the SS20s and of other aspects of the USSR's policy, are not only embarrassments, they are haunting the Warsaw Pact (and NATO) with the spectre of destabilisation. As a result, the USSR has recently become markedly cooler in its attitude to the Western peace movement. It has even experimented with the accusation that Western peace groups are actually serving covert NATO interests in the hope of counteracting the increasing communications between like-minded and non-aligned groups in the East and the West. This accusation is ludicrous — even comic — when Western peace groups are subject to precisely opposite accusations in the West — namely that they are wittingly or unwittingly in the service of the Kremlin — and when they are so clearly causing NATO serious problems. It is clearly important for Western peace groups to act responsibly in the face of the Soviet fear of destabilisation, since anything that causes panic in Moscow would have grave repercussions for the embryonic non-aligned movements in such countries as Hungary and the GDR. Chaos will do nothing to overcome the Cold War; what is needed is a metamorphosis in equilibrium. Nevertheless, the contradictory accusations should be reassuring to peace activists, since they are evidence of the non-alignment and the common identity of the movements in East and West, and also, in a sense, of the common identity of the superpowers that are unnerved by them, in a world where the real imbalance of power is not between East and West but between North and South, between the rich metropolises and the poor peripheries.

The peace movement has made important advances. And in Britain it has awakened a more powerful spirit of resistance than any other political movement in recent years. But its successes must not be overestimated. Not a single missile has yet been dismantled. There is an immense distance to go and the danger of losing a lot of ground before much more is won. In our view, the movement for nuclear disarmament must concentrate more on the questions of alternative policy if it is to avoid demoralisation and defeat.

The image of the peace movement in Britain as mainly middle-class is not entirely true. The same poll that revealed majority opposition to cruise and Trident showed that most of CND's support was in socio-

economic groups C1, C2, D and E (corresponding to the
working class and the lower and middle middle classes),
with more support among women than men. And the
part played by the trade unions in the movement is
extremely important. Nevertheless, a certain stereotype
persists with which many in the most disadvantaged
sections of the British population may find it hard to
identify. For people struggling to have a reasonable life,
without a job, in the economically devastated industrial
regions of Britain, the question of nuclear disarmament
and defence policy may seem abstract and remote in
comparison with the more tangible and immediate
problems of everyday existence. For those oppressed
and demoralised by the dreary prospects that are visible
from Britain's Toxteths — perhaps especially for those
whose daily oppression is compounded by the racism of
the British state, its institutions and its cultural heritage
— the first question must be, what is it exactly that we're
thinking of defending, when so much of our present
situation deserves no defence?

This is an important question (it is the first question in
our questionnaire) and our various contributors have
dealt with it in various ways. For our part, we do not
conceive of defence, whatever else it may mean, as the
perpetuation of the status quo; we — and we believe all
our contributors — are committed to the need for
fundamental change — though the exact character of
that change may be a matter on which opinions differ
somewhat.

Apart from the real danger of a nuclear catastrophe,
which it is obviously in everyone's interest to avoid, the
question of defence policy has an overwhelming
relevance in two particular respects. Firstly, on account
of the economic relationship between military policy and
military budgets and other sectors. How many hospitals,
kidney machines, teacher training courses, renovated
houses or public transport subsidies does a Trident
submarine cost? When so many basic and necessary

services are under attack, and the military sector is being maintained at their expense, the purpose, cost and effectiveness of military policy is obviously very relevant. The second reason is not primarily economic but psychological. It has to do with the relationship between the idea of security and the image the British have of their country and its place in the world.

'Security' is the aim of defence policy. There is of course no absolute security from devastating events. What we mean by security is a *sense* that disasters are improbable, that we are protected from the things that seem to threaten our lives. The things we perceive as threats, however, are not all of the same nature. There are material threats to life such as starvation, disease, war — the horsemen of the apocalypse. In this sense, the majority of citizens in a rich country, at peace, with a basic level of health care and welfare provided by the state, have a real, relative security, at least in the short term, that most people in the world do not have (though in the longer term, the fact that most people do not have it is itself a threat to the 'security' of the minority that do). But apart from the basic material conditions of life, people's sense of security may rest on a great many less objective factors out of which they create their sense of identity — such as their sense of nationality, of history, of having a right to what they have previously taken for granted.

Generally speaking, it is evident that there is a diminishing sense of security and a growing anxiety in the face of perceived threats in both categories. On the one hand, economic factors, unemployment and deteriorating social services threaten people's material well-being; and in the back of most people's minds there must now be at least a vague consciousness of the dangers of nuclear war and ecological catastrophe. On the other, the disintegration of many established patterns of life threatens people's sense of who they are. At such times, people seem to try to compensate for their loss of material security by clinging more desperately to the mythologies and symbols which underlie their sense of identity. When this sense of identity is conceived neither globally nor individually but in terms of a closed nation, culture or race, battling to survive against other nations, cultures or races, there is a danger that nationalistic and authoritarian ideologies will gain power. Such ideologies offer 'security' (illusory and short-lived, as the history of fascism shows) by promising to impose a sense of order, purpose, identity and unity that people otherwise feel unable to create from their own lives. It is at such times, too, that people are most willing to go to war, because war amplifies this sense of order, purpose, identity and unity with the additional binding force of the demand for loyalty to those the war kills — the sanctifying power of human sacrifice.

The Falklands war is perhaps the freshest illustration of this point — in fact of a number of relevant points. It was an unnecessary war which solved nothing in the long term. The territorial dispute remains unresolved and the various possible solutions which might have been negotiated (with or without the full support of the Falklanders) up to the time the shooting war started were, from that time, made impossible by the price that had been paid in young men's lives and the grief of the bereaved.

At the same time much of the potential opposition to the war was silenced by the fear of being disloyal to the dead and of undermining the morale of those whose lives were on the line. Moreover the 'Fortress Falklands' policy that is the result of the war, and which will be maintained at enormous expense until enough of the sacrificial sanctity has worn off to allow the resumption of negotiations, is the very policy that all parties were previously unanimous in seeking to avoid. The Falklanders' way of life, which the war was supposed to preserve, is being permanently changed by the presence of a garrison of troops outnumbering the islanders by three to one.

From the extraordinary debate in the House of Commons on April 3rd 1982, which effectively determined the events of the following weeks, what was at issue, far more than the possibility of the Falklanders pursuing their way of life, was a certain image of Britain and its 'standing' in the world. This image reeks of old imperial vanities which have no place in the late 20th century. It was, as E P Thompson put it, 'a moment of imperial atavism, drenched with the nostalgias of those now in their later middle-age ... ' The image is of Britannia ruling the waves, of Britain as a great power — if not a superpower, at least a military power to be reckoned with, too 'great' to tolerate humiliation.

'Today has put the greatness back into Britain,' said Margaret Thatcher after the recapture of Port Stanley. In her notorious July 3rd speech at Cheltenham, the psychological fossils were even more visible; there were some people, she said, who in their heart of hearts 'had the secret fear ... that Britain was no longer the nation that had built an empire and ruled a quarter of the world. Well, they were wrong,' she continued. 'The lesson of the Falklands is that Britain has not changed ... '

Mrs Thatcher is clearly living in a fantasy world. Unfortunately, she is not alone.

Certainly, many people who supported the war did so reluctantly and because they could see no acceptable alternative, not for Thatcher's reasons, and not with her enthusiasm. But her enthusiasm for the war won a significant response. We mustn't forget this murderous enthusiasm — nor the images and language in which the war was presented in the media. What was important to the war party was the emotional rush, the outlet for repressed sentiment provided by the rituals, whether these were enacted on the dockside at Portsmouth, in the House of Commons, or in the pages of the *Sun* and its sister paper the *Times*, where Enoch Powell put it plainly enough: 'All of a sudden, thoughts and emotions which for years have been scouted or ridiculed are alive and unashamed.' The war was, to a great extent, a matter of mythological theatre.

Mythological dramas, however, serve political as well as psychological functions. The most obvious political effect of this one is the success with which, so far at least, Thatcher has strengthened her own position. Early in 1983, her triumph in the theatre of the Falklands still seems to be counting for much more than the complete failure of her government to create any basis for social and economic reconstruction in Britain; and there is the possibility (scarcely conceivable not long ago) that the Tories under Thatcher will be returned to power at the next general election. Whatever the result of the election, Thatcher's success in retaining support suggests that a significant section of the public is willing to tolerate the kinds of policies which mean the continuing oppression of the most deprived and the protection of the privileged in return for the entertainment and the sense of identity afforded by jingoistic tournaments. One of the factors which has brought this about, and which is hampering constructive political development, is the appeal of a particular image of British sovereignty and British military power which Thatcher has projected , with the help, it must be said, of many of her supposed political opponents. Thus it is that an issue of foreign and military policy has much wider political consequences.

In terms of defence policy, the Falklands war has had other consequences. As a result of the relatively swift military success of the task force, the Royal Navy has retained a role based on a long-range aircraft-carrier force which, not long beforehand, even the Tory government had acknowledged as outdated. Again, this role has less to do with the defence of Britain than with the maintenance of Britain's image as a world power. This raises several questions. Firstly, how much does people's sense of security depend on the idea of Britain as a world power? In most countries, people obviously cannot base their ideas of security or defence in presumptions of this sort. Secondly, is the character of the armed forces primarily defensive or offensive? It is clear enough that a short-range coastal navy such as Sweden's is a defensive force, whereas long-range fleets have a strong offensive potential and can be used as the tools of intervention or imperial domination. As such, they may contribute to the insecurity of other countries, and thus to the insecurity of the general situation. This of course is precisely the problem of the Cold War; both blocs define their own forces as defensive, and the opposing forces as offensive, adding to their mutual insecurity as they expand them. Thirdly, independently of whether countries agree to cooperate to provide 'collective security', the geographical limits of what is being defended need to be defined. Although the Falklanders had been expressly excluded from British citizenship, the Falklands war was presented as the defence of an integral part of Britain. In most public discussion of defence policy, the defence of Britain continues to be identified, or confused, not only with the defence of Britain's surviving overseas possessions, dependencies and strategic footholds, but with the protection of 'British interests' — a far more dubious concept which can be used to justify military intervention elsewhere in the world.

The Falklands war provided us with one other valuable warning, and that was of the suddenness with which a conflict can develop, the speed with which military criteria can take precedence over political criteria, and the ease with which the doves can be caught napping, stunned by the unexpectedness of events and the rapid way that the hawks can draw on hidden resources. As Anthony Barnett has shown convincingly *Iron Britannia*, the task force was dispatched by an inflamed three-hour sitting of Parliament, in the grip of a would-be Churchillian mania which possessed the opposition as much as the government, and in which few dissenting voices were permitted to speak. 'The result was to pre-empt public discussion with a fabricated consensus.' Once the task force was at sea, the rest followed. Each rattle of the sabres made a climb-down more difficult. The morale of the troops and the approaching sub-Antarctic winter were the governing military factors. The illegal sinking of the *General Belgrano* ensured the failure of negotiations.

In our nuclear age, the age of four-minute warnings, it is just such a sequence of events that could bring about the destruction of the planet.

The point from which any move towards an alternative defence policy must start is of course the present position — the North Atlantic alliance and the theory of nuclear deterrence. It is true that many people now have less confidence in both NATO and the nuclear deterrent than they used to. The reasons for this are clear: both blocs have continued to develop, to build and to stockpile nuclear weapons in numbers that far exceed the 'rational' demands of mere deterrence — the ability to retaliate and to inflict unacceptable damage on the aggressor. (Since nuclear weapons cannot be used at close range, the emphasis in nuclear deterrence has been in the threat of retaliation rather than in true defence — the capacity to withstand and repel an attack.) It is therefore more apparent than it used to be that there are more complex and irrational dynamics at work in the arms race and that any process which produces weapons of inconceivably destructive power in greater and greater numbers and which is at the same time complex, irrational and out of control does not in any way contribute to anyone's security.

Moreover the emphasis that NATO thinking now gives to 'war-fighting' concepts such as 'counterforce' and 'flexible response' (which threaten Warsaw Pact forces not simply with the retaliation promised by the doctrine of 'Mutual Assured Destruction' but with the possibility of one-sided defeat) has revealed more clearly some of the paradoxes and the nonsense on which the theory of nuclear deterrence rests. In order to make the deterrent *credible*, a nuclear weapons state has to convince its enemies that it is prepared to use it. One of the most obvious problems is that it is difficult to believe that any rational mind (and it takes a rational mind to be deterred by the threatened consequences of an action) would trigger the deaths of millions of people even in retaliation. And still less rational would it be to initiate a mutually annihilating nuclear exchange in response to a threatened invasion — which would be to use suicide as a means of defence. But we should not stake too much on the rationality of the minds in question. The idea of 'flexible response' in any case is to fog the issue, to make the circumstances in which nuclear weapons might first be used more unpredictable. It is with this intention that NATO has consistently refused to rule out the first use of nuclear weapons by NATO forces. Deterrence therefore now seems to rest not so much on the certainty of terrible retaliation as on *uncertainty* about what might set off a nuclear exchange. And uncertainty, by its nature, makes no one secure. So the dog chases its tail; insecurity breeds more weapons and new weapons, which in turn breed greater insecurity. Nuclear deterrence used to be described as a 'balance of terror', a phrase which suggested a static equilibrium that it was in no one's interest to disturb. In reality there is no such equilibrium. What there is is an arms race — a process in which the antagonists are each constantly seeking a decisive advantage over the other and which perpetuates an instability that is increasingly perilous as the megatonnage accumulates.

With more and more preparations being made for the *use* of nuclear weapons, it is difficult to avoid the conclusion that the nuclear strategists are themselves

losing confidence in the theory of nuclear deterrence. If
they don't trust their own theory, why should anyone
else trust it?

On this side of the Atlantic, this increasing emphasis
on the use of nuclear weapons in 'war-fighting'
strategies has most clearly been seen in some of the
statements issuing from the American side concerning
the possibility of a 'limited' nuclear war in Europe —
linked to the decisions to station cruise and Pershing II
missiles here and to start the production of 'neutron'
weapons. It is this that has been largely responsible for
the growth of the peace movement in Europe and it is
this that has called the very nature of NATO into
question in the minds of significant numbers of people.
For it looks more and more as though the purpose of the
Atlantic treaty is not to protect Europe with American
arms, but to protect the United States with a European
buffer to which a nuclear conflict might be 'limited' — at
least in the minds of American strategists. The
conclusions many people in Europe have inevitably been
drawing from this are firstly that the United States is
willing to see the destruction of Europe in its own
interest — and therefore that Europe has an interest
that no longer coincides with that perceived by the
United States — and secondly that the present nature of
the North Atlantic alliance is contributing to the danger
that the United States might be willing to start a nuclear
conflict in the mistaken belief that it can be confined to
Europe, thereby sparking off a global catastrophe.

But while there is now more scepticism about nuclear
deterrence, more questioning of the purpose of NATO
and, in Britain, more support than there used to be for
unilateral nuclear disarmament, the balance of public
opinion has not yet shifted past the fulcrum. The nuclear
deterrents, Britain's and NATO's, are far from dead.
And what the nuclear deterrent is still seen as deterring
is aggression of one sort or another by the USSR.

Fear of the Russian threat has certainly been used

cynically by hawkish Western governments such as those of Thatcher and Reagan in the hope of distracting attention from domestic problems and forging a sense of national unity against an external enemy. But at the same time as this fear has been built up by Western leaders as a means of manipulating public opinion, the Soviet Union has itself contributed to it by many of its own actions, such as the invasion of Afghanistan, its own continuing build-up of nuclear weapons which, like those of NATO, exist in far greater numbers than are needed for simple deterrence, and for that matter the level of internal repression in the USSR and other countries in the Warsaw Pact. In fact it is a characteristic of the Cold War that the two blocs are locked into the same game, each echoing and reinforcing the belligerence, the oppression and the insecurity of the other in unbreakable cycles of cause and effect. It is an imbecile game the world can no longer afford.

Whether or not there is justification for fearing a threat from without (and, given the possibility of changes in Britain, there is no reason why the USSR should be considered the only possible aggressor), any discussion of alternative defence policy must acknowledge that this fear exists at present. It must also offer either a way of guarding against the aggression that is feared or, alternatively, a way of showing this fear to be unjustified and removing it. Otherwise the policy is unlikely to win public support. This is not to say that an alternative defence policy must be able to *guarantee* that no attack on national territory can succeed. On the contrary, the peace movement must show that today there is no such thing as a guarantee of national security and that all countries' prospects of security rest ultimately not in military strength but in the justice of their relations with other countries, and of the relations between their own citizens. The aim, as Dan Smith has said, must be to redefine national security.

Nonetheless, until the necessary changes in international relations have been achieved, arguments for non-nuclear defence policies must be examined closely. And the advocates of such policies, whether based on conventional forces, territorial forces, guerrilla training, militia systems or civilian non-violent resistance, must show that they can in some way deter, repel or resist aggression. And those who argue that no form of defence policy serves any useful purpose, that all preparation for conflict should be abandoned in favour of peace education and that non-resistance is the only constructive way of dealing with aggression, must, for their part, show that there is some prospect of a significant section of the public coming to the same conclusion — otherwise the preparations not only for war but for nuclear war are likely to remain. The question of feasibility applies to all alternative defence policies and there is a need to discuss not only the merits of the various alternatives but the means of working towards them, not only long-term aims, but also short-term possibilities — the first steps in a better direction.

The questionnaire format of this book is somewhat experimental. There are obviously a great many more questions to be asked than those here and to deal adequately with any one of them would require more than the 3,000 words allotted to each contributor for the entire questionnaire. The intention was not to examine any single question exhaustively but to collect a range of views on some of the central points in any discussion of alternative defence and to arrange them in such a way that they can easily be compared with one another. We have avoided any further discussion of the case for nuclear disarmament only because a great deal has been published elsewhere on the subject and we wish to focus attention on the relatively neglected but inseparably linked issue of alternative defence. So we have asked contributors to accept as a premise that nuclear disarmament is necessary and that 'alternative defence', for the purposes of this book, presupposes the abandonment by Britain of nuclear weapons as well as other weapons of mass destruction such as chemical and biological weapons, and the withdrawal by Britain from any alliance armed with such weapons.[1] This is not quite the same thing as demanding that all our contributors accept the premise of 'unilateral' disarmament by Britain — since we don't wish to exclude the possibility that the nuclear disarmament of Britain might be negotiated ('multilaterally'), for example, as part of the establishment of a European Nuclear-Free Zone. This means that the discussion concerns the defence of a country which, like most nations in the world today, has no nuclear weapons of its own, and no part in any nuclear-armed alliance, but must accept the fact that for the time being other states, including no doubt the superpowers, still have such weapons. For the purposes of this book, moreover, and in accordance with common usage, the term Britain does not include any part of Ireland although a number of our contributors do refer to the present role of the British military in the six counties as a matter of present reality rather than future policy.

The contributors include both specialists in the fields of disarmament and defence and others whose political activity has been concentrated in other areas — including the labour movement, the women's and gay movements, the fight against racial oppression, Scots and Welsh politics and the emerging Green, ecological movement. Again, we hope that the combination of specialist and non-specialist perspectives will help to carry the discussion beyond the rather esoteric circles to which it has been confined.

As the prospects of achieving nuclear disarmament rest largely on the existence of feasible alternative policies, the development of such policies is a matter of great urgency.

Louis Mackay
David Fernbach   March 1983

[1] In fact more than one contributor argues that by remaining, at least for a time, within NATO, Britain can move the alliance as a whole towards disarmament.

**1   The word 'defence' begs many questions,
first of all what exactly is being defended.
Is the defence of national territory ever a
legitimate goal? Do you accept collective
defence at any other level, for example
that of class, race, sex, community,
cultural values or civil liberties?**

Frank Allaun: Yes, collective defence other than defence
of national territory is acceptable, for example that of
class, race, sex, community, cultural values and civil
liberties. But at all times that collective defence must be
non-violent. Almost any other form of defence is
permissible, such as strikes, direct action, conscientious
objection, demonstrations, use of the media. One other
limitation of collective defence is that it should aim at a
specific target and try to avoid inflicting more damage on
innocent third parties than on the enemy in view.

The word 'defence' is constantly misused by
governments. 'Defence' becomes a euphemism for
military preparations — often of the most offensive and
hateful kind. However, writing personally, I would not
call myself a complete pacifist. Some wars can be
justified whereas others definitely cannot. For instance,
if I had been older in the 1914-18 war I hope I would have
had the courage to oppose it in every possible way. Like
Fenner Brockway, the doubts about complete pacifism
sprang from the 1936 civil war in Spain. Until then
Fenner had been a pacifist, but he believed at that time it
was necessary and right for the elected Spanish
republican government to defend itself by arms against
General Franco's military and fascist attack.

Similarly the 1939 war against Hitler was a defensive
war against a fascist nation bent on enslaving others and
perpetrating atrocities on the leaders of the working-
class opposition and on Jewish people.

If a war should take place between the two
superpowers today, I personally would not be prepared
to lift my little finger to fight on either side. The whole
of my limited powers would be to oppose such a war
taking place. A further statement of principle is that a

nuclear war is never justified under any circumstances. To drop a nuclear bomb on another country and thereby destroy hundreds of thousands or millions of innocent men, women and children is not justified in any circumstances whatsoever.

In certain circumstances defence of national territory may be legitimate. I am thinking of the attacks by the South African government on Angola and Mozambique. There can be no doubt that the South African government is launching attacks on these two countries, on their national territory. It seems to me the two governments have no alternative but to use military defence, that is unless they are prepared to have their country overrun by the South African military and returned to a colonialism even worse than that of their previous masters, the Portuguese.

Pat Arrowsmith: I think it's a valid concept outside the notion of nuclear warfare, but there are all kinds of ways in which people can try to protect their basic values without using weapons. I don't know whether defence is really the right word. We haven't got some of those rights that are implicit in the question; they need to be promoted rather than defended. The question really is, what do you do to try and prevent those rights being violated?

I'm not a nationalist, by which I mean I'm not someone who thinks, as an English person, that national territory is important. But I do have to recognise that when you have a whole nation that has been oppressed through the centuries, then it's very privileged for an English person to get up and say that national territory isn't important. If you put yourself in the position of an Irish person, and remember how your nation has been subjugated, you may see the matter in another light. Whereas I wouldn't suggest that anyone should defend national territory with nuclear bombs, I think in the present state of the world there are all kinds of people who have only recently thrown off colonialism — and some who have not yet — who, like black people and gay people and women and other oppressed groups, need to have an identity. So do national groups, and this relates to national territory, unfortunately. In that sense, I don't know about defending it, but I think people have a right to have a sense of being a people in a national territory, at least at this stage of human history.

Meg Beresford: What is being defended? The claim is that our 'freedoms', 'liberty', 'way of life', 'system of parliamentary democracy' as well as geographical territory are what are being defended. Those who champion nuclear weapons say that we need to defend these things from the incursions of an opposite and alien ideology, i.e. communism. What is being defended both externally and internally is the status quo. As a pacifist, I cannot accept any form of military-aggressive defence. There are values of sexual and racial equality and civil liberties which must be protected, but I would argue that to attempt to protect such ideals of human relations by violent means is contradictory and impossible.

April Carter: Yes, the defence of national territory may be legitimate, as it is closely linked to defence of political independence. But there are qualifications to be made: 1) there may of course be economic, political and military forms of domination which undermine a country's independence without challenging national frontiers; 2) in a historical perspective it may be that the close link between the independent state and control over territory is being weakened and we are moving towards a world of overlapping political and social units; 3) it is certainly true that modern weapons make defence of frontiers less relevant than in the 19th century. For all these reasons guerrilla and non-violent methods of resistance are serious options in place of orthodox military preparations; but their inability to defend territory may be a weakness.

Of course some territorial disputes involve pointless

claims to sovereignty, and are a pretext for asserting national prestige; but the real issue then is nationalism, not territory.

Certainly 'defence' of social groups or political rights is justified, and in some extreme cases (for example the Jews under Nazi rule) organised violence in defence of a threatened group is clearly justifiable, whether or not it is likely to be effective. But in most cases what would be involved is political activity, or non-violent protest, and the concept of 'defence' is I think largely metaphorical here.

Stuart Christie: The short and simple answer is yes, but it is very important to define as precisely as possible what one means by 'national territory'. Together with 'national interest' these are usually concepts defined by the state. Working people have to define and defend their interests on a regional, industrial, political and cultural basis. Collective effort is the only way they can defend their interests effectively.

Robert Fyson: Yes, the defence of national territory is, in my view, a legitimate goal: e.g. to take the most obvious example, the defence of Britain against the Luftwaffe in 1940. At the other levels mentioned, except perhaps 'community', 'collective defence' may be a useful concept, but is best pursued by non-military means. I do not believe in the desirability of revolutionary class or race or sex war, and would seek non-violent solutions. Nor do I believe that cultural values and civil liberties are best defended by military means, the use of which tends to erode or suspend such values and liberties. This may sometimes be a regrettable necessity in time of a defensive war against territorial aggression.

Carole Harwood: Defence, in the sense of any *armed* defence, presupposes attack and consequently assumes retaliation; the logic of this is conflict. As a member of the rich, wasteful and exploitative 'developed' world I will not fight the internal battles of capitalism (East or West) in order to further prolong its obscene and parasitical existence. Rather, I am willing to take up an unarmed offensive in order to demolish a system which condemns a third of the world's population to starvation and threatens our whole species with extinction.

By the same criteria I absolutely accept the need for an individual and collective unarmed defence of racial, civil and other liberties. A form of defence already highly developed among the women's movement, involving as it does no violence, little structure and enormous personal commitment — it also appears to be successful.

Ronald Higgins: In the new age of potentially total war it is obvious that we should redefine 'defence'. We have to take account of our unrivalled powers of incineration, and, no less important, our extraordinary willingness to fight wars of mass and indiscriminate slaughter. A nuclear war could plainly be the first (and last) suicidal war.

Wars could once be fought as a rational (if regrettable) pursuit of legitimate interests when political negotiation had failed. Whether modern war of mutual mass destruction could be so used is highly dubious. In this sense nuclear weapons are not really weapons and nuclear war would not be war. Actual resort to them would serve purposes only of retribution or of suicide, *not* of policy.

We must therefore broaden our basic concepts. Security, not defence, is the key. Security involves much more than military ideas. It involves politics (e.g. détente), economics, sociology and psychology. Security is as much a function of mind as of weaponry. It comprises questions concerning fear and reassurance, misperception and its correction, conflict and its resolution. It involves these things nationally, regionally and globally.

Our understanding of security must include the psychology of individuals as well as of nations. What price in interests (or of conscience) are we ourselves willing to pay for how much of it in given circumstances? Security is therefore also a personal, moral and spiritual issue.

Nevertheless there really are bad people and bad governments whose actions must sometimes be resisted with force. The defence of national territory can certainly be one legitimate goal. So is the defence of democracy. And so in principle, is collective defence. (At any level, whether of nation, class, race and the rest.) What *means* are to be employed for what specific purposes in what specific circumstances is the real question for me. Generalisations about this I would consider deeply suspect.

Mary Kaldor: I think that the question of defence has completely changed since the Second World War and the discovery of nuclear weapons. It's not just the discovery of nuclear weapons, it's also the fact that conventional weapons have become very much more lethal. An aircraft equipped with the kind of cluster munitions that Israel used in the Lebanon, for instance, is equivalent in its immediate lethality to a single kiloton warhead on a Lance missile. If we had a conventional war in Europe, it would make the First World War look like a picnic. So in my view, the traditional idea that you need a defence to defend yourself against military attack from other countries, and that you need military forces to pursue political goals, has completely changed. We simply can't have that. Our main objective, whether we have a defence policy or not, is war avoidance. And that's a completely changed situation which I think people haven't come to terms with. How we judge whether we need a defence policy or not has to relate to what we consider to be the best way to avoid a war in the future.

Stephen Maxwell: Is the defence of national territory ever a legitimate goal? Inside this neutrally phrased question there is a more emotive question struggling to get out — how can one ever justify the spilling of human blood over a piece of real estate?

But national territory can never be just a piece of real estate. By definition it is part of a system of international rights and principles. If national territory is invaded then the principle of territorial integrity is challenged and international order is to some degree weakened.

This does not mean, of course, that any action in defence of national territory is justified. International anarchy is not the inevitable consequence of every act of territorial aggression which goes unpunished. The degree to which a particular act of aggression weakens international order is a matter of calculation and judgement. The estimated consequences for the rest of the international system of yielding to an act of aggression is one element in a moral judgement based on the principle of proportionality.

Thus the United Kingdom's military response to Argentina's seizure of the Falklands cannot be justified simply by invoking the general right of a state to defend its territorial integrity. No doubt, as Mrs Thatcher insisted, international order was endangered by the Argentinian action. But by how much? International order does not rest on abstract respect for general rights — which is just as well. It depends ultimately on a complex balance of power and dependence within which each state calculates its own best interest. Had the United Kingdom refrained from military action to recover the Falklands, any tendency on the part of the Argentinians to assume that the United Kingdom would also surrender its claims in the Antarctic — or by the Guatemalans to assume that the United Kingdom would not defend Belize — could have been corrected by timely British measures to adjust the local balance of power of the sort that were so conspicuously absent as the Argentinians prepared their attack on the Falklands. So national territory may be worth defending in principle, but not regardless of cost.

The second reason why national territory may be

worth defending, even at the cost of human life, is its role as a base for the existence of free societies. The principles of national sovereignty and territorial integrity define a presumptive right of peoples to create in their own favour a monopoly over the use of violence within a defined territory. It goes without saying that the existence of the territorial state does not guarantee freedom for all those who acknowledge its authority, even less for all those subject to its power. But without the classic nationalist right of peoples to live under political institutions of their own choosing, freedom would be even more exposed to the arrogance of power than it is already.

Those groups which define themselves as nations are not the only groups which may feel the need to defend an identity. Immigrant minorities, minority language groups, social classes, even the sexes, may feel the need to organise in defence of their identity. At the extreme, a group like Zionist Jews may feel that its identity cannot be secured within the frontiers of the existing state, and take the nationalist road to a separate state: or like the Marxist working class may conclude that it cannot hope to escape from exploitation within the bourgeois state and take the road of revolution. Other groups like immigrants or feminists will seek to defend their identity or group interest within the existing state. There is no *a priori* limit to the methods groups may justifiably employ. The moral status of the different methods of defence, from democratic activity through civil disobedience to acts of violence, is determined as always by a complex process of ethical judgement and the calculation of probable effects, although those groups which wish neither to separate from the state nor to overthrow it are the more likely to accept the state's claim to a monopoly of the use of violence.

Joan Maynard: I certainly accept defence in connection with class, and with civil liberties as well. The defence of national territory can also be a legitimate goal.

Ann Pettit: Yes, 'defence' is something we're a bit squeamish about, isn't it? It's a thought that comes clothed in battleship grey and doesn't last very long in the mind.

Defence ... the whole concept has become so vague that I find it hard to focus my mind on it. Because, of course, with nuclear weapons and as part of a nuclear 'alliance', we don't really need to think about 'defending ourselves' at all, in any sense that's to do with everyday life. One day, we might all burn up in a mass-suicide response to a presumed (would we ever know?) attack. And until that day, we don't have to practise any other form of defence because it's not necessary — it's become all-or-nothing.

Chris Savory: The word 'defence' as usually used today implies use of violence to defend something that is right. Most nation states are far more states than nations, in that they are political, not cultural creations. The defence of a nation state is also implicitly the defence of the status quo within that state. The necessity to defend a nation state also usually arises out of aggression from both sides. So the legitimate defence of a nation state is a very dubious concept. However, it is necessary to collectively defend human rights, the rights of other expressions of life and the rights of the planet. Ideally this defence would employ non-violent methods. We must also work towards resolving the inevitable conflicts that arise between individuals, communities, classes and societies, using methods that do not rely on violence and war. Violent defence is only necessary because we fail to resolve conflicts.

David Selbourne: Most human rights, under every variety of political and economic order, demand the same general preconditions of security for their exercise. Personal and social well-being, however defined, are also dependent upon a minimum level of public and private safety. In addition, fear for (and of) the future knows no

political or economic boundaries. Moreover, as long as
there is no world polity, and no supra-national juridical
order — but, instead, more-or-less homogeneous
national entities within defined territorial boundaries,
historically saddled with rivalries and grievances,
struggles internal and external, and relations of
competition, exploitation and domination — the attempt
to defend national territory and its 'integrity' will
continue; and will continue to be invested with
legitimacy as a part-means to the preservation, within
national boundaries, of what I have called 'public and
private safety'.

This will remain the case whether we like it or not, and
with or without the bomb, however illusory such safety
and reassurance may be judged to be. The issue,
important as it is, of whether it is in fact legitimate to
defend national territory cannot, in utopian fashion, or
because of a distaste for 'nationalism', take precedence
over the facts that national territories are so defended in
the absence of an alternative universal order.

Furthermore, the politics of unilateral nuclear
disarmament is itself implicated with, and arguably
founded on, a defence of 'national interest' — we do not
want cruise missiles or American bases *here* — even
though such a demand has a wider ulterior purpose.
Indeed, it is predicated upon its own alternative
conceptions of national and territorial self-defence,
however vain, in seeking to limit the traditionally
absolute right of the 'nation state' to protect itself by all
means in its power. That is, it remains a national defence
policy, even if such a notion has, in the last analysis, been
made nugatory by the irreversible existence of nuclear
weapons.

The question of other forms of sub-national and
trans-national collective defence — of class, race, sex,
community, and so on — is not a matter of 'acceptance'.
The individual may, of course, seek to deny or escape —
just as he or she may commit individual suicide — social
categories of belonging, or stand back from the defence

of human rights. But they are in each case too closely bound up with individual identity and integrity to be sloughed off by 'choice'. Indeed, the alternative to their defence by collective action, whether violent or non-violent, and whether we ourselves participate in such action or not, would be the gradual dissolution of all human purpose. Among others, it is on these grounds — which contain a moral imperative whose value transcends narrow calculation as to utility or effectiveness — that objections to nuclear weapons rest.

John Shiers: The world to which I am working, as a socialist, is one in which the concept of 'national territory' has no more meaning than, say, local government boundaries in England today. This does not mean that I want to see the extinction of national cultural differences any more than regional ones. On the contrary, we have to work towards a world order where differences between groups are fully respected, and where decision-making power is devolved to as local a level as possible. To fully respect each other, however, we need to have a total commitment to the fundamental equality of each and every one of us. Once this essential equality is fully accepted, and the institutional and structural mechanisms which perpetuate inequality are dismantled, I believe we as human beings will be able to celebrate our differences without the xenophobic and chauvinistic elements which currently divide us.

This obviously sounds hopelessly utopian in the context of our current world order, where we seem to be locked immovably into defining ourselves as part of nation states which are in various forms of competition and conflict with other nation states. I hold enough of a Marxist perspective on the world to view this as the continuing legacy of the struggle to control as much of the world's resources as possible by those groups who hold the levers of power as a result of their ownership of the means by which wealth is produced. In the jargon, this means the international capitalist class. The Western capitalist nation states are each run by a national owning class with close links, growing closer each day, to other national owning classes. They have selfishly channeled the potential inherent in industrial-based economies to end scarcity throughout the world towards amassing vast wealth and power for themselves. They have redistributed just enough of the surplus wealth they have gained to 'buy in' the majority of people in the Western nation states. Through their control of the ideological apparatuses in society they have made it seem to most of us that without their 'skill' and 'expertise' at 'management' (exploitation) we would lose even the gains we have made.

The fact that two-thirds of the world's population are starving or permanently on the brink of starvation is presented as something which we in the West can do little about. Once these poor nations give up their primitive cultural values and become more like us, things will be all right. The more far-sighted representatives of the owning classes realise that the poor nations are not going to put up with this for ever. So, like the Victorian social reformers who pragmatically argued for a better deal for the working class, we have the Brandt report with its arguments to massively increase support to the poor world. This, they hope, will reduce the risk of revolutions which could eventually unite the poor in opposition to the international capitalist order.

In a world as manifestly unjust and unequal as ours is, national conflict is inevitable both between Western nations as their leaders compete against each other for access to more of the surplus, and also between the West and the majority of nations in the world who demand more of that surplus but lack the power to force its redistribution.

Unfortunately the Soviet Union, the only power with the resources to take on the international capitalist order, has long ago ceased to act as a socialist force leading the poor nations and coordinating their opposition to Western capitalist control of the world economy. It is run by a class of bureaucrats whose interest in amassing wealth and power for themselves is every bit as strong as that of the owning class in the Western nations. Their socialist rhetoric is a wafer-thin mask concealing their real nationalist and expansionary ends. They are as much an obstacle to the creation of a genuinely socialist international world order as the Western owning classes led by the USA.

China after the revolution of 1949 looked as if it was set on an internationalist path in the sense of being a spearhead of the revolt of the poor nation states of the world. But its leadership, in attempting to balance national self-interest in a hostile world and international socialism, has increasingly abandoned the latter in favour of the former. There may well, however, still be the potential in the Chinese form of society to act as a genuinely socialist force in a way which is entirely lacking in the USSR.

In these circumstances it is foolish not to expect that most people inside existing nation states will regard national interest as primary. I think the basis for any defence strategy in Western nations must be founded on a total commitment to redistributing the world's resources in an equal and just way. To unilaterally reject nuclear weapons and then simply rearm ourselves with conventional weapons to protect what we perceive our interests to be is no solution at all. We have to fundamentally re-evaluate our participation in the Western international capitalist order and build a domestic and foreign policy which is about its transformation rather than its perpetuation.

Peter Tatchell: Abhorrent though war may be, Europe paid a terrible price for its unpreparedness against Nazi aggression. Many people remember that we were caught napping then and they quite rightly never want it to happen again. If Britain were ever blitzed or threatened with invasion again, there would be strong support, just as in the Second World War, for us to fight a war of self-defence to preserve our right to self-determination and protect our civil liberties and trade-union freedoms.

David Taylor: The current thinking on 'defence' must change. The first atomic explosion precipitated a change in thinking so radical and far reaching that we are still only just beginning to come to terms with its consequences. Humans can now annihilate each other in millions without declaring or fighting a war, let alone crossing a national border. In the past defence has been seen primarily in 'territorial' terms. Historians point to a time when warring tribes fought to defend their territory and conquer that of others; they claim that the same instinct guides us still. The dominant institutions of our society hold this view and defence policy is derived from such an approach. Nuclear weapons are seen as bigger, deadlier and 'better' weapons which can be incorporated into conventional military, deterrent thinking much like any other weapon. However no 'territorial' war can be fought in the modern world. The human suffering and economic repercussions have consequences far beyond simple territorial boundaries and the threat of radioactive fallout makes any war involving a nuclear state a matter of intense personal interest to everyone else.

Secondly, the East-West axis is something of a smokescreen for the real differences that lie between the military-industrial complex in the North and those whom it exploits in the South. It is a smokescreen that hides the real injustices of the world economic order and falsely maintains the illusion of an 'enemy' in the East. Politicians of both East and West divert people's attention from injustice in the world and troubles at home with talk of a foreign 'invasion'. It is a classic case of a no-win situation.

Northern industrialised economies are now so entwined as to make the collapse of one disastrous for the others. Despite all the war-mongering of pro-militarist forces in the United States, their government still sells wheat to the Russians and allows Europe to deal in the pipeline contracts that will assist the Soviet 'war economy'.

The key word in the industrialised North is 'stability'. While their governments are afraid of an outright war with each other, they continue to probe, test and provoke each other by proxy, far from their own borders. They then use the rivalry and troubles as a threat of war (e.g. the 'red menace') and so justify 'defence' and their own aggression.

The concept of 'social defence' has grown out of the rapidly merging interests of those social movements attempting to define a way of life which is not based around the military-industrial complex. It comes from a variety of groups: ecologists, feminists, libertarians, minority racial groups and peace activists. It describes a system of defence that is compatible with our own values of non-violence. It seeks to defend those things which we sometimes confuse with 'territory' — our environment, culture, economic security and freedom of expression. We need to learn how to distinguish between these and 'territorial control'.

All those who witness the exploitation of our planet and her people have a responsibility and duty to act in 'defence', even if this brings them into conflict with the ruling temporal authorities. Social defence doesn't under-value the importance of laws, it simply places our personal responsibility for the welfare of the planet and her people first.

It is easy to see ourselves as acting in 'defence', but in the overview and in the clash of values, it is us, in the peace movement, who are on the 'offensive'. We are directly challenging the patriarchal values which have now gripped the world for thousands of years. We are doing so now with such effectiveness because those values are now threatening life itself. In order to 'defend' life, we have to challenge many traditions that are essentially militarist — a non-violent offensive perhaps? We have to be careful with terms though. Could 'social defence' be used as a safe concept to describe this process?

Dafydd Elis Thomas: The issue of defence cannot be separated from the whole question of the apparatus of the state for it is primarily a defence of the state, and the state's definition of its own territory. The defence of state interests can be construed and constructed in different ways. They may appear crudely as the vested interests of property and capital in the state's ruling class. State interests are often a residual form of imperialism, particularly in an old imperial state whose very basis as a state is imperialistic. Therefore the question of defence and the posture adopted towards other states and nations cannot be separated from the way in which the British state itself has developed as a multinational state which until very recently has deliberately negated its own multinational and multi-cultural character. Suppression of minority nationalities and minority communities both at home and abroad has been a hallmark of the development of the British state, as can be seen so clearly in the continuing war in the north of Ireland. Armed conflict draws its legitimation from allegiance to a state or an anti-state, and this reaches its extreme conflict point when communities within the borders of one state regard themselves as having allegiance to another state, of different territorial boundaries, and to 'defend' themselves create their own community-based armed force. Identifying defence as state activity points of course to the whole question of legitimation of such state activities. 'Freelance' destruction of human life is murder, however state-functioned systematic destruction is legitimated as defence. The basis of the state is violent. In a period of increasing destabilisation and class and racial conflict the willingness of the state to use force internally to defend the status quo is more sharply defined.

It is important not only to identify state activity as being the agency of military action, but also to understand the ways in which the state will seek legitimation for its action, as we experienced last year in the case of the Malvinas/Falklands campaign. The question of the legitimation of state military action is raised very forcefully when we ask the question about the legitimation of anti-state action. Those of us who would argue that it is legitimate for a state to 'defend' itself through the use of armed force when it has been attacked itself by armed force would stress equally strongly that such right to 'self-defence' should be exercised through collective defence rather than individual state activity. In other words acts of aggression should be policed by internationalised forces taking action against aggressive states rather than by individual states taking aggressive action one against the other.

But how would the right of self-defence for states be applied to community or other groups within states? This raises the whole difficult question of the legitimacy of revolutionary action. One possible answer is to suggest that when a section of the membership of the state is attacked in a heavy and violent way by the agencies of law enforcement of the state itself then clearly some form of self-defence for that section of the state's population may be legitimate. The extent of the force used and the likely form of response provoked by agencies of the state through the use of force in resisting the forces of law and order itself is an extremely complex issue. In order to get at the contradictions and dilemmas which are inherent in this kind of analysis we need to demystify the words involved, not only state, nation, democracy, rule of law, law and order, but the whole question of the possibilities of social change, legitimation, and opposition. The difficulty of much of this debate is that it takes us outside conventional British political debate, a conventional debate however which within itself deliberately and continually suppresses the existence of the armed conflict in the north of Ireland, and the more violent forms of opposition and dissent among the black population in the inner cities as well as the sporadic use of violence by Welsh and other dissident groups. With the coming of heavier policing methods, including the policing of 'politically subversive' threats to the security of the state, the traditional rhetoric of liberal democracy, whereby social and political changes take place through electoral procedures in free debate, becomes increasingly problematic. The breakdown of the social-democratic consensus and the deepening crisis of the British economy itself, the increased incidence of racism both institutional and specific, lead to a need to re-examine the military and quasi-military operations of internal and external security, together with the enforcement practices of the state itself.

David Widgery: Nationalism is a nineteenth-century impulse. In the modern world, its main use is as part of our rulers' ideological special effects department — to encourage our loyalty to them against rival nationalisms. The national patch now has its options governed by intercontinental forces: the world economy, the Western Alliance and the multinational companies. Even the City is only one condensing point in the integrated circuit of world capitalism. Thatcher's breathy patriotism is PR; strictly for the Sloane Rangers on Cheltenham race course. Intelligent Tories are only too well aware of its irrelevance to the real world. Nationalism in an old imperial power cannot conceivably be progressive, especially when dressed up as an Alternative Economic Strategy.

The charade of militarily defending 'our' national perimeter against the superpowers is equally irrelevant. The Americans have already invaded and parts of the UK are occupied territory; the Russians are too preoccupied with holding their own people down to take on a bankrupt, cold and riot-prone North Sea island. But rejection of national chauvinism and xenophobia should make us all the more committed to those elements in the national personality which are jealous of liberty, intolerant of tyranny, ethically open-minded and sexually even-handed. And cherish the Brit bits that are respectful of cultural and racial variety and pressing, from below, for popular democracy. The rebel Britain of Luddite breakers and Penbridge insurgents, of Chartist petitioners and Swing Rioters, of the blasphemous apprentices of the Gordon Rising and the sea-green Levellers. The nation, not of the Butcher's

Apron, but of the Welsh Rebeccas and the revolt on the Clyde. The visionary land of Blake and Burns and Shelley, of Orwell and Auden and Orton, of Turner and Whistler and Hockney.The home of Wollstonecraft's *Vindication* and Wilde's *Soul of Socialism* and Morris's *Dream* and Lennon's *Imagination*.

The awful upper-class England of warm gin and tonics in the Members' Enclosure and Advance Commodity Speculators and Harley St face-lifts has got to go. But I'd defend the vulgar, eccentric and unruly country of John Ball's Kent and Wat Tyler's Maidstone and Tom Paine's Norfolk because those values travel beyond frontier and through history. I'd fight for the Cap of Liberty, the Charter, the Suffragettes and the Slough Soviet (and their equivalents in every language and climate of the globe). And those people who carry those sensible, unconventional values today, whether punk rockers or pickets or peace dancers or dreads. It's the political contents not the national expiry date stamp that counts.

2   Defence is traditionally supposed to guarantee national security. Is such a guarantee possible? Given the world's present East-West and North-South divisions, what military threats might a nuclear-free and non-aligned Britain face?

Frank Allaun: There is no guarantee of national security. In 1914 and 1939 Britain was attacked despite the possession of big armaments. But looking at the world today, I see no serious military threat to Britain. Which country would want to make such an attack? The only one the British government can suppose is Soviet Russia. What possible advantage could it give the USSR to wipe Britain off the face of the earth, as it undoubtedly could? First, it would arouse intense world-wide hatred, and second, it would destroy the source of the sophisticated industrial equipment that Russia is willing to buy. Maybe it will be argued that Russia would not want to depopulate us with megaton bombs, but wants to invade and occupy Britain. The answer to that is first, that Soviet Russia has not invaded countries outside her own sphere of influence, e.g. Hungary and Czechoslovakia. As regards Afghanistan, it had already been a communist state for two years before the Russian troops marched in. Sir William Hayter, our former ambassador in Moscow, writing in the *Observer*, said that Russia's aim was 'to prop up a tottering communist regime'. A further argument for the improbability of Russia taking over is that she would have to invade, conquer and occupy West Germany and France, and cross the Channel. The Kremlin has far too much on its plate in keeping Eastern Europe under control, without taking steps so costly in human life and money. Russia lost 20 million men, women and children under Hitler's invasion, and is anxious, I am convinced, to avoid a third world war.

Pat Arrowsmith: This is a question I often speak about at meetings. The truth is that there is, in the real sense of the word, no means of defending Britain against a possible enemy nuclear missile attack. There isn't any interceptor system in this country for bringing down enemy missiles with nuclear warheads. There isn't in any real sense at the present time in the United States or the Soviet Union either. Consequently when people talk about defence they get muddled — they confuse defence with deterrence, which they are also muddled about, not realising the authorities often misuse the term when they are really talking about attack. In World War II (and I was a World War II child) there was actual defence. Civil defence also made sense then. But that's not the position today.

Meg Beresford: If we are to achieve a nuclear-free and non-aligned Britain there will have to be a radical change in our national perceptions. This would necessitate casting off our imperialist past and a less aggressive outlook on the rest of the world. The Falklands war showed these concepts to be very close to the surface in many people and easy to whip up. It should also allow for an unaggressive foreign policy and the necessary development of ways of solving international problems without force. It would require a radically new mentality which could not allow the possibility of force for solving problems.

April Carter: No, national security cannot ever be 'guaranteed' by defence; and in fact political and economic arrangements which minimise the likelihood of military action are usually much more significant than the level of military preparedness. Indeed military preparations may sometimes increase the likelihood of attack by promoting an arms race, pre-emptive strikes or at least mutual suspicion, so the *nature* of a defence policy is important. It should look clearly defensive. The main military threat a nuclear-free, non-aligned Britain would face would be becoming embroiled in a European war, nuclear or conventional. How serious the danger would be depends on whether we can achieve real disarmament measures.

Stuart Christie: Firstly, I am highly sceptical of the claims made by the 'extremists of the centre' as to the expansionist aspirations of Soviet Russia. Russia has made no territorial advances in the West since 1945 and its diplomatic and military advances elsewhere, in an American style 'advisory capacity', have been part and parcel of the power struggle between East and West for leadership of the developing and non-aligned nations. The Russian military and political machine is vastly overstretched as it is. If it were to embark on a policy of expansion it could find its house of cards come tumbling around it and push its borders back to the original Duchy of Moscow. Another unlikely scenario is the re-occupation of Orkney by a revanchist Danish junta. No, the main threat as I see it doesn't come from an external source, although such threats do undoubtedly exist, nor even from internal subversion from the left or the right, but from the 'extremists of the centre' who are now confronted with the natural contradictions of democracy in a highly educated, mobilised and participant-oriented society.

As elsewhere, I believe the main threat to a nuclear-free and non-aligned Britain (which in itself would suggest that the mounting demands for 'accountability' and 'open government' had been effective) would come from NATO and those private back-up organisations which support it. NATO troops may not invade physically — for a time — but they would certainly do everything in their power to destabilise the country and/or contrive a series of incidents to ensure a prompt return to the fold.

A few years ago (1976) the Italian weekly magazine _Europeo_ broke a story which was later supported by the testimony of senior army officers and the head of the Italian and NATO intelligence service, General Miceli. According to a secret clause to the NATO compacts of

1965 all the countries of NATO were to set up 'an organisation composed of trustworthy and capable individuals endowed with the necessary means and capable of intervening effectively in the event of external socialist aggression or internal political upheavals.' Known as the Rosa dei Veinte organisation, this 'parallel' service was set up, according to General Miceli, the then head of the Italian SID and director of NATO security, 'at the request of the Americans and NATO'. Basically, it was a parallel secret service and armed militia who were carefully recruited on the basis of their anti-communist zeal. According to *Europeo*, these anti-communists, all members of neo-fascist terrorist organisations such as Ordine Nuovo and Avanguardia Nazionale, had received training at a NATO base in Alghero, Sardinia, in 1968. All of them, under the control of NATO intelligence officers such as Guido Giannettini and Robert Leroy, were later fully implicated in the wave of fascist terrorism — 'the strategy of tension ' — which has rocked Italy since April 1969. *Europeo* went on to state that this 'parallel' service had also been set up in Britain, Belgium and Germany. It is interesting to note that the Deputy Chief of Staff in charge of NATO plans, operation and intelligence during the period in question was none other than General Sir Walter Walker, KCB, CBE, DSO, who, when he retired as NATO C-in-C in 1972, immediately set about establishing his private army which exists today under the name UNISON. UNISON and other similar little-known anti-communist/socialist organisations such as the Legion of Frontiersmen of the Commonwealth come under the aegis of the Resistance and Psychological Operations Committee, a covert group within the government-funded Reserve Forces Association. The RFA is the representative body of British military reservists and the British component of the NATO-supported Confédération Inter-Alliés des Officiers de Réserve. The RFA was formed in 1970 and is formally an independent organisation, but its 214 members represent all the reserve units of the armed forces. According to Chapman Pincher, close links have been formed with similar units in several European countries, which are actively recruiting 'anti-communist resistance fighters' (*Daily Express*, 18 July 1977). They are also said to have established an intelligence network which NATO chiefs regard as being of great value. (See *State Research* 2, November 1977.)

The Greek coup of 1967 was effected by 'Plan Prometheus', a NATO contingency plan devised in the 1950s to be implemented in the event of an internal uprising. The coup itself was effected by only 300 of Greece's 10,000-strong officer corps, most of them drawn from the elite NATO-controlled unit, the LOK (Mountain Assault Brigade), comprising only 700 men and organised along the lines of the US Special Forces — and directly trained by the Americans. At the time, Colonel Papadopoulos claimed the coup was to prevent the country going communist, but a fortnight after the coup General Pattakos admitted it had been carried out simply to forestall the elections. Also, the known Italian coup plots of July 1964, the Prince Borghese-led coup of 1970, the Rosa dei Veinte plot of 1973, the Edgardo Sogno plot of 1974 — all had identified and inextricable links with NATO and the NATO Secretariat. There were also links between French NATO generals and the OAS putschists in Algiers. I think there is more than suficient evidence to support the thesis that the main military threat to a non-aligned Britain would come from NATO rather than Russia.

Lisa Foley: All defence policies incur risks, but some are plainly unacceptable. This is the basis for rejecting nuclear deterrence, be it mutually assured total annihilation or merely a flexible response. The number of serious risks Britain would face as a non-aligned non-nuclear country would be fewer than what it faces now as a member of an alliance which does not shy away from the possibility of using nuclear weapons first — in fact it is not inconceivable that NATO might pre-emptively nuke Britain in order to 'protect' it from a possible Soviet attack.

The key advantage of being non-aligned is that there would be no obvious enemy alliance threatening Britain. The so-called Soviet menace would be minimised and Britain's world view would no longer be blinded by myopic Cold War stereotypes.

It is therefore essential to our real security interests that Britain goes non-nuclear and non-aligned. This defence policy, like all others, could not offer *absolute* security, nor should it pretend to. Put simply, switching to a non-aligned, non-nuclear policy would be a way of decreasing both the aforementioned risks and threats. And British security policies would be made all the more secure if all of Europe, both East and West, were nuclear-free and non-aligned.

On the other hand, even major transformations of British and/or European defence strategies would not in themselves eradicate other dangers: 1) the problems of nuclear proliferation and nuclear accidents; 2) the ease with which a few determined terrorists could construct and threaten to detonate a nuclear device, thus holding millions of people to ransom; 3) the particularly disturbing trends in American, Israeli, white South African, and to a lesser extent Soviet, military escalation, fortifying ever more ambitious foreign and defence policies.

Despite these dangers, withering away the Cold War alliances and denuclearising both sides' forces would be a crucial turning-point in relieving military tensions.

Robert Fyson: Defence of any kind cannot provide an *absolute* guarantee of national security, especially in a world where the knowledge of nuclear military technology exists. But in the present world of nation states, it is legitimate for such states to seek as much security as possible. (This cannot be provided by nuclear weapons.)

The possible military threats to a nuclear-free and non-aligned Britain would be: a)Soviet nuclear blackmail and pressure for Britain to become compliant with, or semi-aligned with, Soviet policies and interests. (This is more likely than a Soviet invasion, which I discount.) b) American economic blackmail and pressure for Britain to revert to her present position as 'Airstrip One' for US nuclear forces. c) Fallout from a nuclear war in Europe, even though Britain remained neutral. d) Third World nuclear blackmail by, e.g. a nuclear-armed Gadafy's Libya. This is a possibility, but is at present pure speculative fantasy.

All these possibilities exist, and I don't think that we in the peace movement shall do our case any good by denying that we shall continue to live in a very dangerous world, even if CND's immediate aims are achieved. But none of these dangers is as great as continuing on our present course as participants in the nuclear arms race.

Carole Harwood: Whose national security, what national security? While the 'great powers' cynically slice up the world between them on plump knees half hidden beneath the public negotiating table, we are meant to play out their ritual war games on a smaller but imitative scale. This seems to me to guarantee nothing but disaster.

In purely tactical terms it would appear that a nuclear-free, non-aligned Britain would face fewer direct military threats in as much as it wouldn't be an automatic theatre of war. 'Safe' is as unrealistic as the assumption that it would immediately become 'red' (as opposed to the 'white' armies of occupation at present settled in the USAF bases all over Britain?). This perception of 'safeness' is also highly irresponsible. Having made Britain nuclear-free we would then have a moral, political and human obligation to rid the whole world of nuclear weapons. Complacency is the second deadliest sin after apathy.

Ronald Higgins: 'Defence', however construed, cannot of course guarantee national security. There are no guarantees of anything (except death) in this life. Nor can there be solutions of any final kind to the perennial problems of sustaining a basic international order. Utopianism is as silly, and dangerous, in this field as in any other. We have to work step by step, though sometimes boldly, amidst a given set of world realities.

Let me therefore say that Britain cannot become totally immune to nuclear dangers, whether physical or political. No one can; nuclear capacities (or potentials) are now here to stay. So long as we stay.

Britain cannot therefore become 'nuclear-free' in any complete sense. Nor would I wish her to become 'non-aligned' if that means neutral as between NATO and the Warsaw Pact. Granted the right terms and strategies I hope we shall remain a member of NATO. In this connection we must recognise that for the US to unilaterally renounce all her nuclear weapons would be quite a different matter than for Britain to do so. Our renunciation of them could, if carefully handled, make a lot of sense, e.g. in relation to proliferation. For the Americans to do so would gravely destabilise a fragile world order.

Granted these caveats to the question posed, what military threats do I think Britain might face?

i) Outright intentional Soviet aggression is unlikely. But should a war break out between the Americans and Russians either side might find these islands useful. Nor would they respect British, or anyone's, 'neutrality' in a Third World War any more than Moscow respected Finland's in the Second.

ii) Britain could also become embroiled in open military conflict outside Europe, as she did recently in the Falklands. We are not immune to entanglements in the Middle East, Africa or Asia.

iii) 'Military threats' also include political pressures backed by military strength. In the grim arena of

East-West conflict both sides are capable of putting a considerable squeeze on us if we were weak and without allies.

iv) A relatively rich Britain, which we are, must be seen as part of the Rich North by the Poor South. Though an eventual open war between North and South is only a remote possibility we could certainly become entangled in North/South conflicts posing some military/political threat. (This might apply even were we to 'identify' with the South, possibly even more so!)

Mary Kaldor: I don't see Britain, as such, facing any real military threats — unless it be the kind of Falklands-type threat which I think we have to find political solutions to overcome. Mrs Thatcher was very lucky in the Falklands war. We managed to win militarily at very little cost — but I think it was pure luck. I think it was a terrific risk that Mrs Thatcher took and we might have killed very many more people. There are other such circumstances — Belize could be invaded by Guatemala — but I think we have to find political solutions to them now.

The main danger that we would face if we were nuclear-free and non-aligned would be the danger of getting caught up in a war between the United States and the Soviet Union. And that's actually the danger that we face now. What we have to decide, both as regards defence and as regards non-alignment, is how do we minimise the risk of that war happening.

Stephen Maxwell: No defence strategy ever devised, violent or non-violent, has been able to *guarantee* national security. The most secure garrison may fall victim to a Trojan Horse, to human error or venality, or suffer a loss of the will to resist. The most secure defence is one which provides a physical shield against a potential aggressor, preferably in the shape of a geographical feature. But technological progress has reduced the effectiveness of geographical barriers and made the task of building a military shield vastly more difficult. So deterrence has replaced defence as the focus of security planning in the economically advanced states of the world. And given mankind's inherent capacity for acting irrationally, security based on deterrence — on influencing the will of a potential aggressor — cannot be more than a precarious security, or to be less paradoxical, a conditional security.

The risks of a British defence strategy based on unilateral nuclear disarmament and neutrality can be divided into short-term and long-term risks. The short-term risks would arise from the possible reactions of the United Kingdom's own allies. If a government committed to unilateral nuclear disarmament and neutrality was to be elected, the most immediate danger would be intervention by the United States and NATO allies aimed at obstructing the implementation of the new policies or, that failing, at destabilising the government. Although the probability of such intervention is lower than the more melodramatic critics of the United States and NATO will allow, the danger is real enough, particularly if the unilateralist government had been elected, grace of our eccentric electoral system, on a minority share of the total vote. But it is more likely that faced with popular opposition the government would seek refuge in a referendum which would provide it with a democratic alibi for the abandonment of its manifesto commitments.

The long-term risks to Britain's security would be determined by the strategic and foreign policy responses of the United States and the key Western European states. British neutrality, as distinct from unilateral nuclear disarmament, would produce a sharp increase in centrifugal forces within the Western alliance. It would certainly reinforce isolationist opinion in the United States. A United States withdrawal from Western Europe would face its European allies with a cruel dilemma — to go nuclear, individually or collectively, at the cost of abandoning détente and plunging Europe into a new arms race; or to seek a new relationship with the Soviet Union at the cost of increased Soviet influence over their external policies if not their domestic policies. The first would have a serious if indirect effect on Britain's security by destabilising its political and military environment. The second would require Britain and Western Europe as a whole to adjust to a more modest role in international affairs, but provided the political base of the new relationship with the Soviet Union proved stable it would significantly diminish the danger of a nuclear conflict in Europe. Early Soviet reactions and the strength of the European disarmament movement would be among the factors determining which of the two broad responses to British unilateral initiatives Western European states eventually adopted.

The Nordic states would be particularly sensitive to a declaration of neutrality by the United Kingdom. The expansion of Soviet naval power in the Northern seas over the last twenty years has persuaded many Norwegians that they already live behind the Soviet Union's front line. By eliminating the shortest NATO reinforcement and supply lines to Norway, British neutrality would increase Norway's sense of isolation and force her to choose between closer integration with American and NATO defence systems, perhaps to the extent of accepting foreign bases and nuclear weapons on her soil, or herself withdrawing from the Western alliance in favour of neutrality. Either option would threaten the Nordic balance which supports Finnish and Swedish neutrality. Although Nordic politicians would strive valiantly to absorb the effects of British neutrality in a concerted push for an internationally guaranteed nuclear-free Norden, there would be few cheers from Nordic governments for unilateral British moves to neutrality.

Advocates of British neutrality and unilateral disarmament themselves argue that Britain should 'sell' unilateralism and neutrality for reciprocal moves towards disarmament and demilitarisation by other European states. The *threat* of neutrality may have more influence on the policies of other states than the actual adoption of neutrality or the actions Britain could take as a neutral state. Each state will make its own assessment of the implications for its security of the British moves, and given the differing strategic and political circumstances of each state these assessments may not fit well with the plans of Britain's neutralists and nuclear disarmers.

Joan Maynard: I don't think security can be guaranteed. Particularly for a Britain with nuclear weapons. We're a small island with a lot of American bases, which makes us a floating base and therefore a target in any conflict. We'd face far less of a threat if we were non-nuclear. Non-aligned is not possible, for always in life you have to decide where you stand. But to go non-nuclear would make us a lot safer. There wouldn't be the invitation to attack. And in any case nuclear weapons are morally wrong. We should not use them on anyone no matter what the consequences.

Chris Savory: We need not just to 'redefine national security', but to redefine separately our concepts of the 'nation' and 'security'. National security for Britain at the moment means to a large extent securing power for those people who hold power already. It also means the securing of Britain's position of international importance and dominance. The present concept of the nation is a major block to world peace, which after all represents real security for people. The existence of aggressive, sovereign nation states is a major cause of war, and therefore a major reason for military defence being deemed necessary. When governments or the military talk about security, they usually mean securing the freedom of those who have power to exploit those who don't. Real security for people can only be built on trust and strength that come from cooperation, self-reliance, and open and honest communication.

Immediately after Britain had declared its intention to get rid of its nuclear weapons and to leave NATO, the greatest military threat would undoubtedly come from the USA. They would surely try political destabilisation without the overt use of military means, but if that fails who knows what they will resort to?

David Selbourne: 'National security' — particularly if it means immunity from devastating nuclear attack, by accident or design — cannot be *guaranteed*, whether by nuclear or non-nuclear means, as long as nuclear weapons exist anywhere. (Indeed national security has never been guaranteed by conventional means of defence against conventional means of attack, either). And even if the deterrent effect of the existence of nuclear weapons is conceded, the power to annihilate others, whether in a 'first strike' or in retaliation for it, cannot itself 'guarantee' the security of any single individual or nation.

Moreover, since the knowledge of how to manufacture nuclear arms can never now be unlearned, even universal nuclear disarmament and the destruction of all existing nuclear weapons — a wholly unlikely prospect — would make no significant difference to this truth. In fact, a 'nuclear-free defence' is now impossible in any absolute or general sense; as well say a 'knowledge-free' defence, since 'the Bomb' is knowledge, and knowledge of the very properties of matter itself.

It is also obvious that no valid practical or moral distinction can be drawn between the 'protective' value to humanity of the nuclear arsenals of one nation or bloc of nations, and those of another; nor between 'protecting' oneself with one's own nuclear weapons, and being 'protected' by the weapons of others. Neither in the one case nor the other can national security be guaranteed, or even defended.

Furthermore, a nation's manufacture, possession, lack of possession, or abandonment of nuclear weapons are also not — and cannot be — decisive determinants of the general nature of its polity or of the actual geo-political, military and economic interests which it imposes on, shares with, or which are opposed to, those of other nations. (These, in turn, make genuine 'non-alignment' impossible.)

Thus, it is the case that the presence of nuclear weapons on the territory of a particular nation can provide it neither with guarantees for its safety nor immunities from danger. The absence of nuclear weapons also invites no greater — and no lesser — political, military and economic vulnerability than that which already exists by other means and from other causes; nor can it offer any sure exemption from the general physical, political and economic consequences of nuclear warfare anywhere; or from the continuing existence, anywhere, of nuclear weapons.

For all these reasons, a 'nuclear-free' Britain would face, and offer to others, essentially the same threats and dangers as it does already.

John Shiers: Given what I've written in answer to Question 1, it is obvious that I do not believe that defence can guarantee national security. A nuclear defence strategy, far from being the greatest guarantee of our 'national security', represents the biggest threat. This is because of the strategic position of Britain in the 'Western alliance', our being a small offshore island which could be obliterated without possibly even affecting the rest of Europe, and the legacy of quite justifiable hatred which exists towards us as the former leader of the Western capitalist order.

A nuclear-free Britain, however, might still not break with NATO and the Western alliance. In the circumstances of keeping these links, I suspect we would meet a similar fate in the event of a war between the USA and the USSR that we would if we retained nuclear weapons.

I understand why many of the people I most respect in CND, like Joan Ruddock and Edward Thompson, have argued tactically against demanding British withdrawal from NATO. I think, however, such a position could only make short-term gains for CND at a long-term cost. We have to convince the majority of people in this country that becoming nuclear-free and breaking with the Western alliance must go hand in hand.

I do not like the term 'non-aligned' because it suggests we should become neutralist. I think we should oppose with equal vigour both the Western international capitalist alliance and Soviet nationalism with its occupation of East European societies and Afghanistan. We should, however, be 100 per cent aligned with the poor nations of the world and with all rich nations that are seeking a new form of world order which redistributes world resources.

Such a policy would obviously make us highly unpopular with both the Western alliance led by the USA and the Soviet Union. We would be directly at risk from other Western nations attempting to undermine and destroy our independent policies. This is why it is so important for the socialist movement in Britain to work with socialists throughout Europe to build a common, independent, non-nuclear defence policy.

If in Britain a Labour government was elected with popular support for such policies, it would probably be as limited internationally in its scope for action as the Labour-controlled Greater London Council currently is in relation to the Tory government. Such a Labour government would have to work actively with other socialist movements and governments in Europe to obtain support for its policies. It would need to become highly adept at deciding how far it could go in pushing forward its independent foreign and defence policy on its own without provoking forces of retaliation in Europe which could destroy it. All this suggests an emphasis on building an active and live relationship with people, and on political education and consciousness-raising, which has been entirely lacking in previous Labour governments. It is still largely lacking in the current Labour left political practice.

Peter Tatchell: The arms race threatens us all with nuclear annihilation. Our possession of nuclear weapons makes us a prime target in the event of war. As a matter of urgency, Britain must therefore make its contribution to the de-escalation of militarism through our unilateral renunciation of nuclear weapons.

But to win and sustain a clear public mandate for unilateralism, in place of *our* nuclear arsenal or reliance on the *American* 'nuclear umbrella', an *alternative non-nuclear defence strategy* is necessary to placate public feelings of vulnerability to attack from potential aggressors — real or imagined, present or future. And who can tell what the future holds? Because many people harbour quite reasonable fears that so long as there are nations in arms war is always a possibility, credible defence alternatives are necessary in order to win the nuclear disarmament debate.

In the present context, the Soviet Union is popularly held to be a potential military threat. Whether this is true or not, so long as doubts remain in people's minds concerning future Soviet intentions with regard to Western Europe, public support for simple pacifist-inspired disarmament will remain highly improbable.

If major new peace initiatives are to win popular consent, they must therefore go hand in hand with alternative defence options which both put a break on spiralling militarism *and* guarantee that Britain would be able to defend itself in the event of aggression.

Unfortunately, in reaction to Britain's imperialist world role, many socialists and disarmers have simply dismissed any form of defence or military expenditure as immoral and a waste of resources. As a consequence, the British Left, unlike many of its continental counterparts, lacks any coherent non-nuclear defence strategy.

Within the Labour party, this is reflected in a defence policy which merely consists of unilateralism plus cuts in defence expenditure. Welcome as these commitments are, they do not add up to a distinctly alternative defence policy. That would require a much more thorough-going overhaul of our present defence strategy, weapon systems and military ideology and organisation. These still remain deeply influenced by Britain's history as an imperialist great power with colonies and military garrisons world-wide.

The days of simple anti-nuclearism and mere demands for cuts in arms spending are numbered. It is time we moved towards the development for a clear alternative non-nuclear defence strategy for Britain.

David Taylor: This is a rather confusing question. On one level it is obvious that no one can, in the atomic age, give an absolute guarantee of national security. On another, our sense of identity and community will continue no matter how repressive a regime might be. 'National security' conjures up some pretty terrifying images — uniforms, electric shock treatment, disappearances etc. It is also used by politicians as a code word for 'the preservation of our way of life', something that no one is supposed to disagree with. It is a war-time concept used by the dominant institutions of our society to reinforce their own position of power. The second half of this question is also difficult to answer. If we imagine a non-aligned Britain today with all other conditions remaining unaltered (an impossible starting-point), we might see the main threat as coming from the USA attempting to preserve their interests over here. They are highly unlikely, however, to pose an external military threat; diplomatic and financial levers being quieter and more effective. Anyway, 'non-aligned' is a rather negative and bland term for the imaginative and constructive role of a Green foreign policy. The threat from the East has been exaggerated and overplayed, but let's not allow them to call wolf too often. In a fluid political climate things can change quickly and easily.

David Widgery: A nuclear-free and non-aligned Britain is only conceivable after a prolonged and profound struggle against those who at present own and control the UK. The bomb and NATO are not just optional extras but the supreme symbol of the waste and destructiveness of our whole social system. The arms economy has been one of the central motors of post-war capitalism's economic expansion. The Yalta carve-up and the alliances which derive from it block authentic independent development by insisting on the non-choice between a Communist bloc that isn't communist and a Free World that isn't free. So a nuclear-free and non-aligned Britain would have to have undergone some sort of political revolution with the success of a mass movement which would have elements of France in '68, Portugal in '75 and Poland in '81. And we would be under military threat from everywhere where the same process was not in progress.

3 **Would you personally be prepared to kill people in any circumstances? Do you draw a line between acceptable and unacceptable forms of resistance?**

Frank Allaun: Personally I would not be prepared to kill people under any circumstances. Even people I strongly object to, who are dangerous to human survival, such as Mr Reagan and Mrs Thatcher, must never be assassinated. If they were, it would only lead to similar governments by similar people. So a line must be drawn between acceptable and unacceptable forms of resistance. Any non-violent action which could bring down the present Thatcher government would suit me, although I know that because of British history and experience, this is most likely to be done by a general election. A general strike would hardly produce such results. It could win limited demands but not the overthrow of an elected government.

Pat Arrowsmith: I hope I wouldn't. I call myself a pacifist and I'm one of those people who some years ago called themselves nuclear pacifists — that is, people who decided they were not going to support the idea of armed conflict for whatever purpose — good, bad or indifferent, for social rights or anything else — because the potential end-product of any armed conflict was the use of nuclear weapons. I thought that many years ago, and I still think it today. There are certain armed conflicts whose goals I support, like many liberation movements, but I don't support the use of armed conflict because the potential outcome of this is the use of weapons of mass destruction. Also I don't think you best achieve humane ideals like socialism by using means that contradict them.

Meg Beresford: No, I would not be prepared to kill people in any circumstances. For me the only acceptable forms of resistance are those of active non-violence.

April Carter: I do draw a line between acceptable and unacceptable forms of resistance, but it is not precisely on the borderline between non-violence and violence, though it is politically important to extend the scope of non-violent action and reduce resort to violence. I would be very reluctant to kill in any circumstances, and I'm not sure whether I could bring myself to do so in reality; but as I would be prepared to support certain kinds of armed defence, I can envisage situations in which I might.

Stuart Christie: As an anarchist I am bound by my social and political beliefs to a mode of working that reflects and furthers those beliefs. As to killing people, I think the line I would draw would be that dictated by common sense. I don't think I would hesitate to shoot anyone threatening the lives of innocent people if it appeared to me obvious they meant to carry out their threat — or someone with their finger on the button that would trigger off World War III. On the other hand, knowing what I know now, I doubt if I would have become involved in a plot to assassinate General Franco in 1964. The years between 1936 and 1945, perhaps — but 1964, no. I should add that the mere fact I was arrested and sentenced to twenty years for what I did probably achieved more for the anti-francoist movement in terms of mobilising world opinion than killing Franco would have done.

Lisa Foley: Out of necessity and as a last resort I would kill to protect myself and others in self-defence. I would consider the possibility of using violence to further revolutionary struggle. On the other hand, it would be politically irresponsible to engage in military struggle which wasn't likely to succeed: resistance would have to be tempered by what seems possible.

Inhumane weapons like napalm are repudiated by international law, and rightly so. Certain targets, e.g. hospitals, are deemed unacceptable. War itself is morally inexcusable, but on some occasions politically necessary.

Robert Fyson: Yes, I would be prepared to kill people in some circumstances, especially to stop someone else killing my family or me. As an extension of that principle, I might volunteer, or accept conscription, for a military force fighting against an aggressor. This might include a civil war, e.g. the Republican side in the Spanish civil war, but I don't believe any such eventuality is likely in Britain (see my answer to Question 10).

Carole Harwood: I can envisage being personally prepared to kill in circumstances where 'life or death' choices have to be confronted at an immediate and personal level — i.e. no premeditation, no delegation, and no way out.

Ideally, however, a moral imperative should necessarily prevail though the arguments can become highly complex, not to say abstract. For example, should one be prepared to kill oneself? At a very basic level, if a driver of a car that has gone out of control finds that s/he is hurtling towards a defenceless pedestrian then surely s/he should avoid the pedestrian even at the risk to the driver's own life, simply because the driver is at a massive physical advantage. Should this perception of responsibility begin to inform the policies of governments, it would become obvious that the weakest and most vulnerable are always, by nature of their position, the 'strongest'.

Should the driver survive and decide to abandon the car for a bicycle, then real progress would have been made!

If living 'defenceless' means no longer being party to the illegality and immorality of probable genocide, then I personally am willing to take the risk.

Ronald Higgins: Yes, I think there *are* circumstances in which I would be prepared to kill, albeit with horrified reluctance, if only to reduce the numbers likely to be killed or, perhaps, enslaved. My fantasy in this connection is defending African families in a South African civil (or 'liberation') war.

I would however certainly draw a line between acceptable and unacceptable forms of resistance. For a start 'resistance' might include offensive action, e.g. air raids on undefended cities of little military significance. The use of force must always be proportionate to its aims. Likewise I think the non-use of force must be proportionate to its likely consequences.

Mary Kaldor: I would not have been a pacifist during the Second World War. I think I would be prepared to kill people in some circumstances. At the moment I think that's just unbelievable, but I can imagine myself killing Nazis. I can imagine myself resisting in certain situations in the Third World.

Stephen Maxwell: I can imagine circumstances in which I would consider myself morally justified, indeed morally obliged, to kill one, or more, of my fellow human beings. Pacifism is committed to the proposition that the deliberate killing of one human being is an absolute evil, which carries the absurd entailment that the killing of one hundred people is no greater an evil than the killing of one person. The moral status of an act of killing is determined by the balance between the evil represented by the killing on the one hand and the evil represented by the consequences of not killing on the other.

There are no *a priori* grounds for excluding any form of resistance. Those acts — and only those acts — of resistance are justified which, when all the probable consequences of action and inaction are considered, promise to minimise the quantity of evil. Non-violent forms of resistance are subject to the same principle of proportionality as violent forms of resistance. The extent of the deprivation, suffering or coercion caused by non-violent resistance has to be balanced against the moral value of the desired end. Where the resistance is violent, the degree of pain or suffering inflicted by the *act* of killing must be assessed along with the quantity of evil represented by the *fact* of death. While no form of resistance can be rejected *a priori*, the extent to which the form of resistance adopted undermines those rules of behaviour which operate *in fact* as general restraints on behaviour is an important element in the choice of form of resistance.

Joan Maynard: I'd find it extremely difficult to kill anybody, but you never can be sure. We had to resist the Nazis in the last World War, but then we produced the Nazis, we helped to build them up. For me it would be very much a matter of last resort, and I'm not sure even then.

Ann Pettit: Yes, I might be prepared to kill individual people, in very special circumstances — if I or my children were threatened by a loony, if I had a weapon that could kill a torturer and release his victim. But I think that organised military means tend inevitably to pervert ends, and are therefore self-defeating. Will life ever be 'normal' for the Falkland islanders? When regimes aiming to establish material equality are established after a long armed struggle, do they in the end create the kind of societies they wanted — or does the 'armed struggle' leave too many scars behind for peace to flourish? I honestly don't know the answer to these questions; I suspect I might think very differently if I lived in Namibia, El Salvador or Afghanistan.

Chris Savory: I would never premeditate the killing of another person. I don't know what might happen under sudden and unexpected threat. I believe that whenever possible, resistance should be non-violent. But I don't believe in moralising about other people's violent resistance if there is no credible non-violent alternative being put forward. Violent resistance can be understandable but not acceptable.

John Shiers: Yes. I think unfortunately that as long as violence provides the bedrock of power which is used to back up unequal relationships, the use of violence in retaliation is inevitable in certain circumstances.

If one individual violently assaults another, it is usually necessary to use equal or greater violence to stop the attack. There may be possibilities, however, which minimise retaliatory violence for people trained in non-violent methods of resistance. Violence, however, even to the point of killing someone if necessary in self-defence, has to be accepted as a sad reality of life.

In relation to resistance against groups or classes who exercise self-interested power over others, there also has to be recognition of the right to use violence in self-defence or to overthrow injustice when no other means are available. I entirely disagree, though, with the position held by the generation of revolutionaries influenced by Frantz Fanon, who argued that the violence of the oppressed is a cleansing and therapeutic process, restoring a sense of pride in people whose identity had been colonised from them. Once violence becomes an end in itself, the oppressors have won, because their punishing and hierarchical values have become part of the collective psyche of groups resisting their power. Violence breeds violence. The foundations of a democratic, collective, non-hierarchical society can never be built on military discipline, terror or violent intimidation.

Where possible, I believe that oppressed groups and classes should develop non-violent strategies of resistance because these are inherently anti-militaristic and rely on self-conscious mass action. In societies where power is exercised wholly by force or domination rather than manipulation of democratic machinery, the scope for non-violent resistance is clearly limited. Usually it will have been tried in the past and crushed, embittering the next generation of freedom fighters.

Where violence in pursuit of social justice is made inevitable by the actions of the national ruling class, I still consider moral considerations are important. Even if all concepts of morality are class-based (and I do not think they are), it simply is not in the interest of an oppressed class to allow itself to become so embittered that it lives for the day when it can torture and kill its oppressors just like they are now torturing and killing the resistance. Our morals must be superior to theirs, otherwise we simply become like them when we gain power. The experience of virtually all revolutions to date tells us this.

I am aware that it is easy to say this writing in the still relative tranquility of the current political situation in England. I have no experience of my sisters and brothers in the movement being ruthlessly tortured or executed, or a foreign power occupying my country. But I take inspiration from the fact that in Nicaragua today there is a revolutionary government which has fought against the most brutal and corrupt ruling class imaginable, and is still faced with organised attempts by the US government to undermine and destroy the revolution by the most violent means. The movement in Nicaragua has learnt from other revolutions in the past and has actively worked to minimise the use of violence, both in gaining and keeping power. Its minister of state Tomas Borge, who was himself tortured by the Somoza government and whose wife was murdered by Somoza's agents, says clearly and unequivocally: 'If we take revenge, we destroy the purpose of the revolution. Our revolution represents the renunciation of revenge.' Every independent observer who visits the country says how remarkable it is that this principle is being carried out in reality. That gives me hope!

David Taylor: In all honesty, I don't know. There is violence within me and I cannot emphatically rule out the possibility that some day, under some circumstances, I might kill. Does that prevent me from really understanding non-violence? What's to stop even that small acceptance from escalating when confronted with a greater violence? I believe there is an untapped source of strength in complete non-violence; surely we are aiming, ultimately, for a vulnerability that allows us to be open with each other, to share our feelings and knowledge at a much deeper level. We have a task to transmute violence in society, both personally and in our institutions, but we cannot deny that we must live with it.

Dafydd Elis Thomas: Whilst I have a strong respect for the pacifist position I no longer feel able to endorse it personally. There are situations when the use of force is the lesser of two evils. This is not to accept the theological arguments for a 'just war'. Though I believe it is possible in certain circumstances to support the concept of a 'just revolution'. This is precisely the moral and theological dilemma faced by many of the theologians of liberation writing in Latin America. The alignment of Christians with anti-fascist forces in the thirties and forties, and the present alignment in Latin America, are such as I would find very difficult to question. Forms of resistance are directed to a specific situation in which oppression occurs. The resistance is an attempt to overcome the oppression. For the Christians and humanists in El Salvador or in the ANC in southern Africa the institutional violence and oppression of the regimes under which they live can only be matched with a liberative violence. Such a stance is of course problematic but the absolutist stance of resisting all forms of violent resistance is itself equally problematic, in that it tends to deny the existence of violent structures. Pacifists will of course take the view that non-violent resistance can be effective in dismantling violent structures. The decision as to whether violent or non-violent methods ought to be used in a particular context is itself a difficult one, but I would not be prepared to condemn out of hand those who within the context in which they operate can only see a violent solution as 'viable'.

Ruth Wallsgrove: Killing is wrong, but...

Islington Women Oppose the Nuclear Threat, of which I'm a member, was not formed as a pacifist group, but to bring out the connection between male power and nuclear weapons; between, for example, the desire of some men to terrorise women in their homes and on the street, and the desire of some men to hold the lives of millions of people in their hands. As feminists, we resist being victims; we can't believe that it is better to be killed than kill, or encourage other women to believe this. And yet killing someone is an extreme act; who is entitled to judge that, in a particular situation, killing someone is a more liberating act than not killing them?

To tackle the question at all, we had to work on a real example, a local Islington situation rather than a national liberation struggle:

A woman that a couple of us know had been beaten up by her husband over a period of years before she heard of the local Women's Aid Refuge and could leave him. After she moved into the refuge, her husband — who had money — hired men to find out where it was and watch it, to collect evidence that she was an unfit mother and that he should have custody of her child. In this he didn't succeed, but he did persuade the court to allow him access, with the proviso that he was not to have her new address but to collect and return the child from its nursery.

This was more than two years after she had left him. One day he rang the nursery on some excuse — the child was ill, and had to go straight home — and got the address off them. Taking the child with him, he went round with a meat hook and acid. In front of the child he stabbed the woman nineteen times. Only the action of the woman's neighbours — also women from the refuge — saved her from the acid and death. They hit him over the head with a broom, stunning him and giving her time to crawl into the next-door garden. The police actually came pretty quickly and arrested him. Then — and this is really the punchline — he was prosecuted for grievous bodily harm and given a two-year sentence.

Those of us that knew her wished he had been killed instead of stunned; for now, in less than two years, he'll be able to pursue her again. It's not the first time he's tried to kill her — how can we believe that it'll be the last? And he, unfortunately, can't be dismissed as an isolated madman; there are several more who've killed or tried to kill women from that particular refuge.

We wished it had been done, even accidentally; pursuing him in cold blood, as he has pursued her, is no solution. The police and courts can't protect her; to keep him locked up for ever would only be another way of killing him. Only changing society so that men like him don't grow up believing they can do as they please with women would solve the problem, in the long run, if not for that particular woman, and that's what we all work for. But — would it have been wrong to kill him? Would *you* have wielded the broom, or a heavier object, knowing that you might kill him?

I'm sorry to say that, as a group, we had no answer to that. Our reactions ranged from one woman who thought that she would have done it, especially if she or a friend of hers had been under attack — that 'my guts would go for survival' — but that it would never be *right*, to one who felt that she couldn't stand it, but she couldn't tell another woman not to do it.

If we found this difficult, how would we deal with armed struggle, with killing strangers? This man must be held 'responsible' for his murderous actions, if any of us are responsible for anything; but can a member of an opposing army, perhaps a conscript, be held equally responsible? Obviously some men join armies because they relish the idea of wielding power, but — in contrast to the slow, steady, life-long education men get about 'standing up for themselves' — armies often have to subject their soldiers to concentrated brainwashing to make them feel all right, or at least blank, enough to kill. And this brings us to another point; anyone who resists armies by force must also mess their heads around, to distance themselves from the individuals they kill and the consequences of killing, from the very thought that killing is what you're doing when you fire a gun at someone.

And yet we cannot tell the Eritreans to resist non-violently in the face of Ethiopian machine-guns, in the face of a genocidal state immune to (and largely removed from) world opinion. What can we say to the Black people in South Africa who feel they have tried non-violent resistance? How could we have resisted Nazi Germany other than by force, knowing (as people knew) that they would murder people if they invaded (before non-violent resistance could be effective)? We could say — as some do — that we ourselves will not kill, but we won't oppose armed struggle for liberation in the Third World. But then we have the luxury to take that stand, a luxury surely denied to those in countries like El Salvador where the government doesn't care if it mows down innocent civilians.

However, we know that everyone — even the Thatcher government in the Malvinas — calls it self-defence.

What it came to, for us, was that we could hate killing as a strategy, but we could not hold to a principle that judges, say, the Eritreans and El Salvadoreans as being *as wrong as* the British military. However slippery the slope, however uncomfortable it is to do so, we *have* to make political judgements based on our understanding of who has power in a situation. Those of us who wouldn't have wielded a heavy object against the attempted murderer would have campaigned that any woman who had done so should not be convicted of murder — knowing, anyway, that she'd probably have got a heavier sentence than he would have done if he'd succeeded in murdering his ex-wife, since woman-killing (going by the sentences men get) is taken as a less serious crime than man-killing in our society. We would not have mourned the death of the Yorkshire Ripper, I'm afraid; we would not be unhappy if Ronald Reagan somehow 'disappeared'. Our stomachs all turn at bombs of any sort, the plastic explosives of the IRA and PLO too — but we can't see them as the guilty parties, ranged as they are against armies with a million times more money and resources.

In women's campaigns in this country, at Greenham Common as in the struggle against male violence of a more individual nature, we certainly feel violence would be an inappropriate strategy; killing one innocent bystander, or indeed even someone not so innocent, would be not merely an act of brutality and ugliness but tactically suicidal, and therefore wouldn't save women. We live in a society where liberal opinion doesn't 'see' state violence, won't even oppose the Malvinas war, but only 'sees' the violence of 'terrorists'. But we're not presenting ourelves as 'naturally' non-violent because we're women; and we're *not* offering ourselves as martyrs. To sum up our answer to the question — but not by any means to end the debate in our heads — I offer two points. Firstly, we deny that men are 'naturally' violent, and therefore male-dominated society must take the blame for bringing men up to be killers. Secondly, we will not publicly criticise the weak who fight back against the strong, the Eritreans or El Salvadoreans or even the IRA, but will campaign to make people see that the cards are stacked against all of them by rich states that glory in their military power, and not call killing foreigners or 'terrorists' something other than murder. We can't bow out of our responsibility to judge what is truly self-defence and what is not, and we can't tell the oppressed they're not to fight for their lives. Killing *is* wrong — but the guilt, first of all, lies with those who have power.

David Widgery: Yes. Especially if that someone was intent on killing me or someone I cared for first.

4 Attitudes to militarism have been rather mixed on the left, except among pacifists. Many people who in principle are opposed to militarism have found themselves accommodating a degree of militarist outlook in relation to national liberation movements and the defence of 'revolutionary' states. Is it possible to pursue any sort of armed defence policy without contributing to militarism?

Frank Allaun: It certainly is possible to pursue armed defence policy without contributing to militarism. The neutral countries of Sweden, Switzerland and Austria all have military forces but can hardly be accused of militarism. There is some doubt in my mind as to whether they are wasting their money on weapons. These neutral states would be as secure today if they had spent no money at all on 'defence'. There is no doubt that if Russia or any other country wanted to invade them, they could be beaten. So the 'defence' forces are a waste of resources.

Pat Arrowsmith: It's a difficult question. I've just said that I don't believe in killing people in the cause of socialism, justice etc. Looking at the situation in individual countries — and I suppose the one I've been most involved with (I think quite correctly as I'm English) is Northern Ireland — you can see that if one supports the political goals of, say, the Republican movement, it's hard to imagine how they can be achieved by means of non-violent resistance, because this has been attempted and has not in fact succeeded. And anyway the nationalists are numerically the minority. So there's a problem. At the end — or perhaps at the beginning — of the day, people who don't believe in killing are taking an ethical stand, I think. You say (as indeed a vegetarian says in a slightly different context) that you're not prepared to do a certain thing: you consider it absolutely wrong, consequently you have to seek other methods of achieving the just goals that you have in mind.

Meg Beresford: No.

April Carter: The problem here is to clarify what militarism really means — it's a rather cloudy word. I think some form of armed defence is possible without jingoistic nationalism, extreme glorification of the military, or political and cultural domination by the military. But any armed defence implies some status and power for the armed forces and fostering military values: either among a sector of the population, or in a system of universal military training having some concept of citizens in arms. Whether this is pernicious probably depends quite a bit on how armed forces have been used in the past, whether the society is democratic and peaceable, attitudes to authority, etc.

Stuart Christie: That depends entirely on the social and political motivation of those involved and the organisational structure of the defence force. Traditionally, guerrilla and liberation movements have had most success when they are fighting on their own territory and in defence of their class interests. The danger of militarism arises when a conflict develops between obligations to one's comrades and the society of the outside world. Also dangerous is the abandonment or suspension of normal moral and social considerations. Only a soldier of the nation state or of a marxist-leninist or corporate state claims to be released from personal morality on taking his or her oath of allegiance. So far as anarchists are concerned, the manner in which we carry out our tasks is as important as the task itself.

Safeguards can be built in to ensure the armed forces remain defensive in concept. The defence units must be democratically structured and seen as an integral part of the community, sharing common goals — not something grafted on by an external authority or under the control of any political party or organisation. Instant unquestioning obedience would be superfluous in a well-managed and democratically controlled defence force.

Robert Fyson: By 'militarism' I understand essentially the glorification of war and the martial virtues. It is not easy to pursue an armed defence policy without *some* degree of militarism, but we should aim, by emphasising a purely defensive security, to reduce the level of militarism to the minimum, even if it is not possible to abolish it completely.

Carole Harwood: 'Militarism' in this context seems a suspect term. In most national liberation struggles a military convention has been forced upon women and men actually engaged in opposing 'militarism', and in this sense I think the question performs a deceptive glissade. While recognising the need for Third World countries to organise and conduct their own liberation struggles, it should be remembered that anti-colonial wars could effectively be waged on the home territory of the colonial power. For example the radical opposition in the United States certainly contributed to the ending of the Vietnam war. Any people represented by a government committed to waging a colonial war has a duty to obstruct and oppose that government's policy. To do otherwise is to sanction such policies. We shouldn't expect half-starved peasants to fight our wars for us.

As regards the defence of 'revolutionary' states it is perhaps necessary to make certain distinctions between the armed defence of a country like Nicaragua and the armed-to-the-teeth protection of 'socialism' paraded in Moscow. The former is threatened, the latter has become threatening; and while the danger of militarism may be considered nascent in any regime which relies on guns to hold power, even to defend its own freedoms, the militarising of a collective mentality is a conscious and inhumane act.

Ronald Higgins: The form of this question itself indicates how confused and perhaps prejudiced we have become. The military constitutes an honourable profession, certainly when it accepts the necessary democratic constraints. Militarism is a distortion of the necessary military function, an excessive reliance on military responses or the idolising of macho power.

We do not have to choose therefore between pacifism and militarism, whether in relation to liberation armies or anything else. We do have to choose between non-violence and controlled military violence. An armed defence policy as such need not contribute to militarism. I saw little sign of it amongst the millions of my fellow countrymen who fought to defeat Hitler and Tojo. Most of them were very glad to return to their lawn-mowers. And, incidentally, to a modest silence about their sacrifices.

Mary Kaldor: I believe strongly that the next stage in the evolution of humankind has to be to overcome militarism. I think the Left has very often been bemused and confused by militarism. And I think that people have very often identified socialism with what is actually militarism — and that the Soviet revolution did us a great disservice, in the sense that it justified the use of force and statism. And we've tended to confuse socialism with statism. As regards the Third World, it may well be that for very poverty-stricken peasant communities, statism is a step forward compared with the situation they're in at present. Nasserism, for instance, I regard as a progressive force. But for us in the West, where we've made certain major achievements with bourgeois democracy, I think any form of statism — and particularly military statism, which I regard as an extreme form of statism — is a step backwards. I think this will be one of the big struggles on the Left — between the internationalist, libertarian, anti-statist Left and the more militaristic, nationalistic, statist Left. Some people call it the struggle between isolationism and internationalism.

Stephen Maxwell: As an ethical system militarism is the promotion of military values. As a principle of social organisation it posits a determining role in the political and social sytem for the military leader or military caste.

Probably any form of armed defence involves some glorification of military values. If the state cannot convince its soldiers that it is sweet to die for one's country it must at least persuade them that it is noble and worthy to do so. Yet there are examples of countries committed to armed defence which avoid any deliberate glorification of military values and in which the military professionals are accorded no special status. Switzerland, a neutral country whose defence system is based on a citizens' militia serviced by a small professional military cadre, is a notable example. Sweden is another. Two NATO members, Denmark and the Netherlands, also support sophisticated defence establishments without giving rise to a cult of militarism. By contrast, Britain and France cultivate a military mystique and encourage their citizens to identify the armed forces as representatives of the most cherished values of the nation.

Joan Maynard: I think it probably is. Particularly in relation to Northern Ireland. The resistance movement there — which some people describe as terrorist — is opposed to the military occupation of their country by us. Another thing about Northern Ireland and what used to be Southern Rhodesia, now Zimbabwe, also countries like El Salvador today, is that they have no way of changing their government by democratic means. They can either submit, fight or they can use some form of passive resistance. But you need a more highly developed society for people to accept that.

Chris Savory: Military force is always justified by saying that it is defending something that is 'right' — e.g. 'democracy', 'the revolution', 'the true faith', etc. Or it is attacking something that is 'wrong' — 'communism', 'capitalism', 'fascism', 'unbelievers', etc. You don't need to be a pacifist to see that to justify killing on the basis of

subjective perceptions of right and wrong is to tread on
an extremely dangerous moral tightrope. So, if a
military 'defence' is seen to be an end in itself, it is
sustaining militarism. On the other hand, during the
transition from a nuclear weapons-based defence to a
non-violent defence, there will be a short-term need for
an armed defence. If the end of militarism is perceived as
a goal and a non-violent defence policy is desired, then a
military 'defence' can be part of the process of demilitari-
sation.

David Selbourne: It is not possible to pursue any
effective policy of armed defence without 'contributing
to militarism', particularly given the 'sophistication' and
firepower of alternative non-nuclear weaponry. But in
the epoch of the threat of extermination by nuclear
armaments, we can no longer retain the category of
'militarism' without internal discrimination and
differentiation.

'Conventional' militarism, however vicious, which
does *not* threaten the extinction of the human species,
nor the destruction of targets, non-combatants and
assailants together, cannot simply be equated — morally
or politically — with forms of warfare which promise to
do precisely this. Moreover, the fact that competitive
militarism itself can be said to have brought the world
gradually closer to the point of catastrophe is not in itself
ground for subsuming the less lethal within the greater,
or more nearly terminal, forms of threatened violence.

No arms can be used, or even carried — except for
ceremonial or theatrical purposes — with wholly pacific
intent, meaning or consequences. To argue that they can
is to adopt precisely the same false ingenuousness of the
nuclear arms-mongers who pretend to the maintenance
of world peace and an equilibrium between nations (by
means of the 'balance of terror'), while in fact pursuing
their own ruthless *Realpolitik* for competitive advantage.

nuclear free defence
genbach

10/13/83 10/27 2 dur 150

inland/heretic
0946097 046

633

4/28/78

Cummings, Mary

34 Fairfield

Buffalo

832-3529

John Shiers: I think it is possible but very difficult. The experience of the anarchists in the Spanish civil war is hardly an inspiration to those of us on the left who believe there is a real alternative to conventional hierarchially structured military organisation.

David Taylor: Can one limit one's definition of militarism? Does it include the need for hierarchy and discipline? All armies will generate their own militarism, because it is this mystification of war that makes the illusion palatable — this includes liberation as well as conventional armies. As long we accept the need for some armed resistance, we have to accommodate a degree of militarism, but we certainly shouldn't tolerate the degree of militarism around us now. The pageantry, medals, uniforms, films and toys — they all instil in us, from childhood, the belief that war can still, after all these years, be glorious.

Dafydd Elis Thomas: Answering this requires a definition of militarism. Militarism presumably means supporting a culture of violence and military activity for its own sake rather than for social ends. Clearly all military activities have within them incipient forms of militarism and to the extent that all states and all liberation movements that resort to armed force have a military mode of operation they can indeed find themselves maintaining a form of 'militarism'.

David Widgery: 'Militarism' is a dustbin word which is largely useless. Anti-militarism is, unfortunately, a tradition monopolised by the abstract utopians on the British Left. And because it doesn't require you to do very much, just 'be' and hold the odd jumble sale, it manages to be simultaneously moralistic and ineffectual. Which probably accounts for its manifest unpopularity among the pragmatists of British Labour. But the (equally starry-eyed) habit of giving not-very-critical support to any old state that announces that it is socialist is even more destructive. Starting in the Stalin-infatuation of the thirties, through the Mao-cult and now continued as farce by orthodox Trots, it creates the disastrous impression that the Left is prepared to justify conditions for the working class in the so-called socialist world which are in some respects worse than those we fiercely denounce in the capitalist democracies. The working classes may have educational failings but they are very good, and quite experienced, in spotting hypocrites. The sad lesson of the Left in the twentieth century is that unless one is scrupulous in evaluating the social content of other people's revolutions one ends up negating the case for one's own. As for the ultimate Left-militarists, the individual terrorists who came out of the defeats in Italy, Germany and North America in the early seventies, they are liberals with guns. They cause very little real inconvenience to the modern state compared with even a minor strike, and provide a convenient excuse for it to enlarge and improve its own armed nuclei.

5   Alternative defence proposals cover a
    wide spectrum. At the least radical end is
    the retention of a strong conventional
    force and perhaps even membership of a
    de-nuclearised NATO. At the most
    radical end are policies based on 'civilian
    defence', i.e. organised but non-violent
    resistance. In between there are various
    possibilities based on territorial forces or
    a citizens' militia. There is also the view
    that aggression is best dealt with by non-
    resistance. What kind of policy do you
    advocate, would it have a deterrent effect,
    and what are your comments on the other
    approaches?

Frank Allaun: It is largely a waste of time to consider
what form of defence Britain should have until we have
dispensed entirely with our nuclear weapons. That
means: no cruise, no Trident, no Polaris, no American or
British nuclear bases on our territory. That is such a big
step forward that I am not certain it is very profitable to
consider what should take their place.

I am strongly opposed to those who want to spend
more on conventional weapons, as Dr David Owen
proclaims. I accept the Labour party policy which is that
Britain should reduce the proportion of her GNP
devoted to arms to that of the other West European
countries. In 1981 I asked John Nott, then our Defence
Secretary of State, how much that would save our
country. To my surprise he gave me a precise answer:
£3.6 billion a year. At present prices, that would be well
over £4 billion a year. That money is desperately needed
for housing, health, education, re-equipping our
industries, and for aid to the hungry nations. This
government has so far refused to answer the question:
why should Britain, a relatively poor country compared
with many in Western Europe, have to spend a higher
proportion of its GNP on arms than those governments
do? I appreciate that people, or a majority of them, want
reassurance that there is some kind of defence against

foreign attack. Though I am not advocating disbanding the armed forces, my own view is that they serve little good purpose, but I do believe that the British people as a whole are not yet ready to accept that view.

However, some 'civilian defence force' would be a mistake. I would say reduce our conventional forces as outlined above. That in addition to ending our nuclear forces would be a second enormous step forward. The proposal for organised, but non-violent, 'civilian defence' is mistaken. The kind of men it would attract would be the more bellicose and reactionary type of our population. It might well be used for strike-breaking or other purposes quite different from the declared intention. Moreover, like civil defence, it would recruit large numbers of men and women who might believe they were defending their country but were in fact being prepared for a third world war. To create such a force would be to accept implicitly that another war was inevitable, which it is not.

Pat Arrowsmith: One of my difficulties about this question is that I wear a number of hats. As a pacifist (and I define that term as non-violent opposition to injustice) I can only say that I believe in non-violent resistance, with all that that means — quite militant non-violent resistance. As somebody in CND (and I think many pacifists are in CND wearing that hat) I take a sort of intermediate stand. I would very much welcome this country deciding to abandon nuclear war strategies totally, consequently consider another kind of defence. I'm a member of Labour CND and it's been considering this question. So, wearing that hat, I have to consider whether there are various types of defence which do involve killing people but which could have some bearing on the abandonment of nuclear weapons strategy. I suppose, looking at it wearing that hat — not a pacifist one, not what I consider my actual hat — I can see that various kinds of home defence, as it's sometimes called, and partisan defence — guerrilla warfare — could perhaps be a substitute for nuclear war strategy. Even certain kinds of conventional armies, such as Switzerland and Sweden have, could be. But there is always this possibility, I think, which is why I became a pacifist, that any conventional war could escalate into being nuclear. What I don't accept is that this country, or any other, can remain in a nuclear-based alliance like NATO yet claim to be non-nuclear. Take Canada; it doesn't have any nuclear weapons on its soil but it has warning systems that are part of the whole nuclear weapons strategy. And it's proposing to test cruise missiles. Then take Norway — a country which doesn't have actual nuclear weapons on its soil but remains in a nuclear alliance so is likely to have them hurried in at a moment of crisis. It would still be a major target were there to be a nuclear war.

I really think that in the nuclear age people have to think of quite different ways of defending — or better, protecting — important values. If it's a question of a possible invasion by an enemy power which would subvert values that are really accepted by the population as a whole, then people have to think about this. There are examples, in relatively recent history, of non-violent action that has been taken to defend values, or even to promote them. This is some cause for encouragement. As far as I know, no war has achieved its ends without a good many unpleasant things that may not have been intended occurring — suffering and so on. No conflict has been resolved satisfactorily by totally non-violent means, but there have been various encouraging examples, some of them in occupied countries during World War II. These do indicate the potential for achieving objectives through total non-cooperation. And I think when pacifists talk about non-violent resistance, what they really must mean is determined non-cooperation, which can include economic action like boycotts, industrial action, strikes — quite militant strikes — picketing, occupations, refusing to obey orders — like the teachers in occupied Norway. And this can really throw the occupier — it did in Norway under the Quisling government. So if you're looking for ways and means of preserving values that any particular group or nation thinks are worth preserving, then you should try to find some means of preserving them which is not totally at variance with the ends you have in mind.

Meg Beresford: I would advocate the use of active non-violence in concert with tactics like non-cooperation, boycotts, mass civilian resistance, as advocated by Gandhi or Martin Luther King.

April Carter: What I would ideally like is a Britain relying very largely on non-violent methods with small armed forces with a policing role (e.g. fishery protection) and for use by the UN. What I am willing to advocate as first steps are a conventional military defence of Britain, and membership of NATO conditional on it becoming substantially denuclearised. I think the case for non-violent resistance is becoming stronger and needs to be put, but it is not yet convincing even to the great majority in the nuclear disarmament movement, and one can only shift opinion gradually.

Stuart Christie: One definition of war is that it is 'an act of violence to compel our opponent to fulfill our will'. Nation states are born in violence, for the most part relate to each other through violence and maintain their power and privilege through violence or the threat of violence. If there were some viable non-violent method of overcoming or neutralising an enemy without causing bloodshed not only pacifists but squaddies would be overjoyed as well.

I would advocate a two-tier defence policy — a standing army and a Community Defence Force based on a local and industrial level. A standing professional army would act as a front-line defence force in the event of external aggression.

This outstanding defence force would, of course, be structurally different to the present army and would be run by Soldiers' Councils. It would be organised on three basic principles: voluntary enlistment, an electoral command structure whereby all commanders are elected by units (each basic unit being small enough to work out its own fluid command structure), and self-discipline whereby rules for discipline are drawn up by the Soldiers' Councils and generally approved and ratified by all units. The disciplinary rules would have to be observed on the basis of individual responsibility and awareness of the possible results of ill-discipline on one's fellow soldiers and the community one is defending.

There is a lot of nonsense talked about anarchists balking at providing leadership in a situation where immediate decisions have to be made. In small units the relationship is similar to that between a musician and a conductor, or a nurse and a surgeon. Even in much larger groups a similar relationship can exist between commanders (not officers!) and men as witness the defence of Madrid in 1939 by the National Council of Defence coordinated by the anarchist bricklayer Cipriano Mera, commander of the IV Army Corps.

An anarchist would require that all defence units should be independent of orders from external sources, except in the case of overall strategy as agreed by unit coordinators at platoon level. The basic defence unit should comprise small groups of 5-15 persons, loosely grouped in a non-hierarchical fashion into platoons of approximately 100. These units would be responsible for organising their own training and identifying targets and local objectives as well as running their own intelligence-gathering and counter-intelligence functions. It would require, however, all intelligence to be pooled in the data banks of a unified computer system with compatible terminals and a common operating procedure.

It would also be essential to avoid any tendency to organise along conventional military lines — to group into large battalions under a general staff subject to decisions based on possibly questionable political or military expediency, or to 'party' or 'popular front' type control. Apart from avoiding the temptation to engage a superior army in conventional-style warfare which could at worst lead to defeat, or at best unnecessary losses of people and equipment, it would, more importantly, ensure that political power remained with the rank and file and did not pass to the centralised leadership of a party as happened with such disastrous consequences during the Spanish revolution in 1937.

I am certain a democratically structured and popularly controlled two-tier defence force would have the desired effect of dissuading any prospective belligerent from any act of aggression. Apart from the enormous cost in manpower and resources involved in having to fight every inch of the way against an enemy which encompasses the entire population and maintaining lines of supply to an army of occupation, there is also the destabilising effect in the home and other occupied territories of properly conducted psychological warfare on the aggressor's military forces and civilian population. A people who place their entire confidence in an army which is then defeated are easily demoralised, subjugated and exploited.

Lisa Foley: We could imagine a better-than-life scenario in which Britain along with the rest of Europe joined in a movement to split the two blocs. The movement rejected all dependence on nuclear weapons and took no 'shelter' from either superpower's nuclear umbrella. The European nations declared themselves non-aligned and devised non-nuclear defence strategies appropriate for each country's needs. A general strategy of 'defensive deterrence' was espoused. The nuts and bolts of the particular defence policy would differ greatly between each nation, though.

Britain, for example, might be likely to have a strong coastal defence backed up with a modest-sized navy; in contrast, a landlocked, mountainous country might opt for in-depth territorial defence. Britain is not well suited for rural guerrilla warfare because of its fairly flat and heavily urbanised terrain and dense population. Urban guerrilla warfare serves to blur the distinctions between civilians and combatants and may be morally unacceptable in most circumstances for this reason. Non-violent resistance may be morally appealing and has the potential to be adopted anywhere and by anyone, yet it would definitely be inappropriate for confronting certain kinds of warfare, e.g. aerial attack.

It is impractical to choose the best alternative defence approach without knowing the context the policy was being framed in. The assessment of threats and the special priorities of each government would weigh in heavily.

Robert Fyson: I favour the retention and development of conventional forces, and indeed, perhaps even membership of a *denuclearised* NATO, which would be very different from the NATO we have now, The ideas recently advanced by Frank Barnaby for a high-technology conventional defensive deterrent, without any need for conscription, seem to me the most fruitful line to pursue.

I would not rule out a territorial force or citizens' militia in case of enemy occupation seeming likely, but I don't think this in itself would deter aggression; and it could be argued that it might indeed spread an element of militarism more widely among the population.

Non-violent direct action as a means of political protest, e.g. currently against cruise missiles, has something to be said for it. But again I don't believe it could deter an aggressor.

Carole Harwood: Historically humankind has shuffled and ambled towards the very edge of extinction on the one hand and the possibility of 'sunlit uplands' on the other; to choose the latter means finding a new way to live for all the inhabitants of our planet. Central to survival is the creation of a hegemonic peace, and neither a 'strong conventional force' nor a 'citizens' militia' seem to me to go any way towards shifting the balance away from a mentality of violence. More toys for more boys?!

The argument is circular. Who and what are we supposed to be defending? Does it seem entirely logical that the less privileged classes of the privileged power blocs should form ranks in preparation for slaughtering each other in order to protect the sectarian interests of international capital? As for a citizens' militia, history suggests they learn the traditional values of conventional armies (rape, looting, etc.) with disturbing speed.

Why fight fire with fire when water is more effective, why not oppose force by its opposite — organised non-violent resistance and disobedience; in short 'active peace'?

As to the 'deterrent effect' — haven't I heard that phrase somewhere before?

Ronald Higgins: The choice of defence policy must depend on the context, including the degree of responsibility taken for residual colonies, small dependent states, e.g. Belize, and for allies or neighbours, e.g. Eire.

In some contexts each of the possibilities you have mentioned, including non-violence, can be effective and justified. At the other end of the scale I could not honestly recommend to Washington, Moscow or Peking that they unilaterally renounce all their nuclear weaponry. For any one of them to do so could invite major instability, even war.

In Britain's case I find the arguments for continued membership of NATO very strong. But it needs to be progressively de-nuclearised; ideally NATO might become able to retain only a minimum US strategic deterrent based in the US and at sea. (Eventually humanity may prove clever and wise enough to create an internationally organised ultimate military sanction strong enough to resist any two of the three superpowers at the same time. Nothing less will allow total nuclear disarmament.) A refashioned NATO would first of all renounce the foolish and dangerous doctrine of 'flexible response' and create a battlefield-nuclear-weapon-free zone ideally on both sides of the

East-West border as recommended by the Palme Commission. There could then be a progressive reduction of other European-based nuclear systems. NATO would however simultaneously ensure that its conventional, especially anti-tank, forces were entirely adequate to meet any plausible Soviet conventional attack. Recent weapon guidance technologies offer good hope of this.

NATO should also be geared to defend Western Europe in considerable depth so as to *absorb* and envelop any Soviet attack. There would be a useful role for territorial forces, a citizens' militia, pre-trained guerrilla forces and civilian non-cooperation within this strategy. I do *not* think these means would be adequate without powerful regular armies, and full air and sea support.

If we are to reduce and finally remove nuclear weaponry from Europe we may even need to *increase* defence expenditures for a while. A nuclear world is a serious place: there is no free lunch, especially for Europe. Incidentally, most of public opinion does, and rightly, take defence seriously and is, I think, unlikely to allow defensive arrangements that are any less robust than the kind I have sketched.

Mary Kaldor: In the light of what I've said, I think the task for the Left is to overcome the use of force in international relations. And that means, I think, not that we have to think of alternative defence policies, but that we actually have to think of how to wither away defence. And that puts me in a rather peculiar position on the Left because I think many of the radical policies — even the non-violent civilian defence resistance strategies — are actually totally unrealistic. On the other hand, at the other end of the spectrum, I think just substituting a strong conventional defence for nuclear defence would make the risk of war possibly more likely, anyway just as likely. I think that one can't have a war in modern times, whether or not it involves nuclear weapons — and the likelihood is that it would eventually involve nuclear weapons. So my own view of what kind of a defence *countries* should have — and I'm not at the moment confining this to Britain — is that one should have a non-nuclear, low-level defensive conventional force. I wouldn't say that we should get rid of conventional arms altogether — because I think that also is unrealistic. It's not on politically, and although I don't believe that defence policy means much in terms of avoiding a war in military terms, it does mean something in political terms.

Dan Smith has used the term 'defensive deterrence' — the idea of a conventional defence policy which emphasises defensive elements, and doesn't have offensive elements like strike aircraft, tanks, aircraft carriers. The aim is really to exact a high admission price, to make it clear to an enemy that it would be very costly not only in military and human and economic terms, but also in political terms. The idea of the defence policy is that you are trying to build on international political constraints that already exist. So, for instance, you make it clear that it would be very much worse to invade Britain than it was to invade Afghanistan in terms of the whole political status you might have in the world. So the aim of such a defence policy would really be to make it difficult for potential aggressors. There's no such thing as a foolproof defence. If any country wants to bomb us to pieces, they can. And that's something we've really got to come to terms with. Therefore the only way to avoid attacks is political; and it may be that a defence policy has some such political role.

Stephen Maxwell: The United Kingdom should adopt a policy of armed neutrality. Its armed forces should include a powerful defensive air capacity and anti-submarine capacity. Its ground forces should be based on a system of citizens' militia, with the adult population as a whole trained in techniques of non-violent resistance. These measures should be supported by a major programme of civil defence against nuclear war.

Such a policy would have a limited but significant deterrent effect. It would give the United Kingdom the capacity to inflict substantial damage on an aggressor and to impose high costs on an occupier. Clearly it would *not* supply the ability to deter a nuclear attack. In a world where the number of nuclear states will increase whatever the UK does, that must mean a more modest role for the UK in international affairs. Even Margaret Thatcher might have hesitated to send an expeditionary force to the Falklands had the Argentinians been able to arm their bombers with atomic weapons. Three points should be made about the vulnerability of the United Kingdom itself. It is highly improbable that the United Kingdom would face threats of nuclear attack except in the case of a wider European, or a global, conflict. In neither case would a neutral and non-nuclear UK rank as a prime nuclear target. Furthermore thanks to the civil defence programme the British population would enjoy a significant level of direct physical protection against nuclear attack.

Joan Maynard: Again this is a question of how far you can carry the majority of people with you. At this stage I think most people will want to keep conventional weapons for defence. And I stress defence rather than retaliation. Even in war with conventional weapons, lots of people get killed, it's hellish. And at the end you have to sit round a table and talk.

Jonathan Moore: Given the assumption that the people of any particular national territory have the right to defend their political and social destiny, the question to be answered is: how is the defence of this right to be achieved? If a gap emerges between the individuals in society and the political-military structures which have arisen with the ostensible purpose of defending that society, then a grave weakness has occurred in the realities of defence. Indeed it would seem in Britain today that such a gap has widened, as political and social progress continues, to a point where the military system is almost completely divorced from the dynamics of society; that the political and military minorities of society have taken over themselves the defence of the state without any proper consensus of the people of the state.

To be effective in defence any future political-military structure charged with the purpose of defending a territory must bridge this gap. This is essential if that structure is to involve the widespread participation of the population. This is not an original statement, indeed when Confucius was asked what were three essential conditions for the pursuance of a successful war, he replied: 1) the support of the people; 2) arms; and 3) food. When asked which condition he would give up first, he answered: arms. When asked which condition he would give up next, he answered: food.[1]

All military structures are a result of concepts of war drawn from a particular territory's military culture which is 'fundamentally a development of the assumptions and values peculiar to the society of which it is part'.[2] That being so, military change will necessarily involve political, social and cultural changes. This is essential if the new structures of defence are to be based on popular participation. It is paramount that a common agreement upon the broad political aims to be achieved must be arrived at if a defence policy and any serious attempt at altering the defence structures is to be made.

It is patently clear from any realistic and informed analysis that Britain's conventional military structures are unable to perform the task of the defence of Britain. The alleged conventional superiority of Warsaw Pact forces of about 3/1 against NATO should not be in any way alarming, if NATO conventional forces are sufficiently competent. German forces in the Second World War were able to succeed with a greater inferiority against both Russian, British and American troops. It would appear that this is a crux of the problem,

1   As quoted in M Elliott-Bateman, *Revolt to Revolution* (Manchester, 1974), p 305.
2   M Elliott-Bateman, *Defeat in the East* (Oxford, 1967), p 29.

resulting in the need for tactical nuclear weapons to cover organisational incompetence, rather than as a legitimate defence. It is claimed that the removal of tactical nuclear weapons could only be compensated by a vast increase in conventional weapons and manpower. This is disputed; what *is* needed is a vast increase in combat effectiveness which would require a considerable change in present military structures. Since existing structures are sacred cows (and this is the main crux of the problem), we finish (and probably will be finished) with nuclear weapons because if military structures won't change neither will their function — and this has scarcely changed since 1942. We forget basically that both British, Russian and American successes against the Germans from 1943 onwards were based upon overwhelming superiority which compensated for lack of combat effectiveness.

Clearly, if Britain is to move away from a reliance on nuclear weapons, a new approach to defence is needed. However, any new system of defence must provide a *realistic* deterrent. It must be functional; possessed of a real war-fighting capability, able to resist and defeat an aggressor numerically greater than itself.

The idea that loosely organised militias or 'guerrilla training' provides an easy answer to the problems of deterrence is nonsense. For example, any study of militias during the Russian or Spanish civil wars proves that unless militia units are highly organised, well trained and disciplined and operate in conjunction with more regular forces, no amount of enthusiasm or political fervour can be a substitute. To imagine otherwise is to court disaster.

The guerrilla is faced with similar problems. His struggle does not automatically succeed. Often the best that can be hoped for is a stalemate between the opposing sides. What frequently is misunderstood is that in the classic examples of guerrilla campaigns (China, Vietnam) the guerrillas were successful because they operated as part of a sophisticated military system with regular and semi-regular mobile strike forces; all of which formed part of a major political and social movement. Clearly any new military structure, if it is to truly possess a real deterrent capability, must provide effective resistance, to escalate the cost of aggression to an unacceptable extent, and most importantly the capability to expel an aggressor completely in the final stages of the war.

A structure which would provide Britain with the strongest form of non-nuclear defence could be classified as a citizens' militia/mobile force system:

Such a structure cannot exist in a vacuum; it is dependent upon the total support of the 'unarmed' people, that is, the citizens' complete opposition to an aggressor. Based on their complete belief in the superiority of their own social stance, this results in their willingness to carry out non-violent and passive resistance. It is only in these circumstances that 'non-violent' resistance can be effective. The role of the 'unarmed people' would be general opposition to the enemy, intelligence gathering, sabotage, etc., creating the correct conditions and circumstances in which the militia and mobile forces develop and operate. It means, even if overrun, the population would continue to carry out this form of resistance according to the conditions of each locality.

The components of the armed forces would be based on a militia of small, territorially located units, with a universal right and duty on the part of all the population to serve in some organised capacity, be it medical, pioneers, engineers, police, fire brigade, underground newspapers, or couriers. Service would be a prerequisite of citizenship. Such a system would provide a huge force of life-support organisations and militia units with the role of direct local defence of their particular areas, in conjunction with local mobile strike forces. The nature of militia operations would usually be of the defensive and guerrilla type; particular emphasis is placed on the guerrilla role because to put lightly armed militias in defensive battle against a better equipped and trained opponent is usually to court defeat. Generally, the militia would protect their own localities, support mobile strike forces, and if overrun carry out harassing and guerrilla operations on the aggressor's rear. The great strength of a militia is that it provides a breadth, depth and resilience to absorb shock which is impossible to achieve with other types of forces, even a cadre/conscript army. Only the massive use of resources on the part of an aggressor can hope to overcome such a system backed by a determined and organised population.

Finally, operating amongst the militia, it would be necessary to possess a mobile strike force with the task of carrying out regular mobile operations against an enemy, transforming the capability of the militia to resist at a local level into decisive military action at the national level to expel the aggressor, and to which end it would be equipped and trained. The need for such a force has been recognised by all countries that employ a militia system. In the cases of Switzerland and Sweden, the 'field corps' make up the largest proportion of available forces. It is unlikely that such an emphasis in terms of the ratio between mobile and militia forces would be necessary, indeed possible, in the case of Britain.

The presence of mobile forces at regional and national level combats the problem of 'localism', the major weakness of a decentralised militia system. The mobile forces must be recruited from the militia in general, and still trained and organised on a part-time basis, though this would mean a greater commitment of time in training, etc. for its personnel. It would only become 'regular' in times of crisis or emergency. To retain a large 'professional' cadre or full-time units outside a crisis is to produce a division in values, outlooks, and attitudes between the two systems. This would be divisive and lead to a compromising of the democratic and participatory nature of the militia, and increasing dysfunction throughout the system.

From such mobile forces, elements could be drawn to fulfil any alliance obligations felt necessary or to serve as part of UN forces. However, the air and naval power possessed by the militia, together with their mobile strike components, would, due to Britain's geographical location, produce a capability for limited force projection involving contact with neighbouring states and their armed forces. So in this respect, Britain's military capability would be of a more extrovert nature. And no doubt should fulfil a role in defending the Western shipping lanes to Europe, etc. Though this is the only real forward capability possessed by the militia outside the European theatre.

A militia system could provide a counter-measure to any nuclear blackmail attempted by other nations, a scenario commonly used against arguments for non-nuclear defence. A militia would provide the people of a state with the armed and organised capability to resist the enforcing of policies by a government under threat of nuclear blackmail. Without a complete monopoly of armed force it is unlikely any government could achieve such policies against the will of the people. Naturally risk is involved, but the capability by the population to resist such nuclear blackmail exists. Especially as the nature of a militia makes it impossible to knock out or paralyse by selected nuclear strikes on bases, installations and lines of communication, which regular and cadre/conscript forces are very vulnerable to.

As briefly sketched above, in such a structure the greatest deterrent comes from the organised armed commitment of the people of a state to defend themselves against aggression. The commitment involved shows a far greater will to resist than purely the amount of money a nation is prepared to spend on the salaries of 'professional' soldiers and their increasingly expensive equipment. It should also lead to a political-military policy that is one with the people of the nation, and thus halt the general and growing feeling that a political and military 'professional' minority are managing the citizens of this country to their graves.

Ann Pettit: I stomp about from little meeting to little meeting proclaiming that, contrary to what is said by the cold-war re-armers, dropping the 'nuclear' component of our defence does not mean we are having to drop our defences. 'What about the army, the navy, the air force?' I say — implying that for the time being, at least, I'd accept a trade-off of nuclear for conventional defence. And so I would if it would lift the immediate threat of Armageddon. I also think that 'alternative blueprints' have a limited value. Ideas about defending ourselves should come from people everywhere talking about the subject, and thus coming up with ideas. At the moment, I don't think most people in this country would accept the notion that a non-military way of defence could be really effective. Yet it could be, of course. In the face of total non-cooperation from the people of a country, there is little a ruling group — whether they be native or foreign — can do.

I think the peace movement will reach as far as its ideas, and those ideas reach very far into the future — to a world where military defence is fast becoming a boy's game of the past. In a way, 'the deterrent' has helped give birth to this vision. But we are talking about hundreds of years, and meanwhile we are here, now, with a debate about defence we have created and with very few positive answers to the question people everywhere ask — 'But we've got to defend ourselves, haven't we?'

One possible transitional strategy could be to see the armed forces in all sorts of other ways than purely to do with killing. They are already used as manpower in emergencies, but this could be dramatically extended. Just think — our army, instead of reinforcing their macho brutality on arid manoeuvres in Rhine forests and British bogs, could be employed as part of a United Nations force that would descend on areas of the world where disasters had occurred, or where some large-scale development was needed (tree planting on desert fringes, irrigation, clearance, etc.) and — just help, just work at what needed doing, whether it was erecting a tent city for earthquake victims or lending their equipment or training in small-scale engineering techniques. If this were to happen, people would be brought closer together by seeing armies as being helpful (literally) rather than as brutes ready to blur distinctions between 'military' and 'civilian' people. And the young men in the armies themselves might become humanised, rather than de-humanised.

Elaborating the fantasy now, why not replace the notion of armies for training in killing by some kind of 'peace service' — a year or two paid by the state for which all young people were eligible to volunteer, as a kind of vastly extended IVS? They would go to work alongside local people anywhere in the world, where help was needed. Maybe there would, for a while at least, have to be one army, with guns and helicopters and ... tanks? They seem so dinosaur-like, somehow (not when they're coming down your street, pipes up a Pole somewhere in the head), and that army would be the United Nations army. Its role would be strictly peace-keeping, and it would have a monopoly of all the weapons. Oh dear, look what I've argued myself into now! They'd use their monopoly to get to be the most powerful group in the world, and terrorise everybody else.

Chris Savory: I would advocate a policy of organised non-violent resistance, because I believe non-violence to be right, and because I believe that if it is properly organised it can be effective.

To discuss 'deterrence'. 1) We have to assume that there is no deterrence against irrational destructive violence. This is the case whether we possess nuclear weapons, conventional weapons or no weapons at all. 2) Deterrence based on the threat of large-scale destruction of the 'enemy' is very destabilising, as it leaves no room for compromise. 3) Deterrence as a concept is shaky because it depends on the aggressor's perception of a situation. Military adventures are undertaken with the idea that they will be successful. The fact that many are extremely unsuccessful shows how wrong perceptions can be; but this knowledge doesn't stop wars.

More important than a deterrent is the pursual of

policies designed to reduce the reasons for Britain being attacked, alongside the development of a defence strategy that could actually be effective against aggression (unlike nuclear weapons) and that could be effective in resolving conflict. It is a total delusion that war solves conflict.

Military defence just invites an arms race and military attack. It will always be possible for an enemy to try and obtain the military capacity to overcome you. What then is your response? To keep building up 'defensive' weapons? When would it stop? That situation would be aggressive; if people felt threatened and they still relied on military methods it would be very easy to slip back into building up 'offensive' weapons.

Modern technology and the real possibility of genocide makes non-resistance unacceptable. Modern military defence is based on high technology and highly trained personnel — what place would territorial forces or a citizens' militia have in a military defence?

David Selbourne: My basic premise is that genuine — as distinct from cosmetic — nuclear disarmament, whether unilateral or multilateral, is not going to take place on any militarily significant scale in the foreseeable future; or, much more likely, at all. (The deployment of nuclear weapons may, at best, be marginally impeded, but that is a different matter.) Any realistic, non-utopian, discussion of the subject, including discussion of the necessity for resistance both to the spread of nuclear weapons and to an 'invader' must be conducted — in my view — within this assumption.

The nuclear powers, like any domestic ruling class, will not disarm voluntarily, nor ever come to trust each other sufficiently to disarm *pari passu*. However suicidally, 'security', 'deterrence' and the politics of increasingly intense rivalry for world domination will continue to be (allegedly) promoted by the manufacture and possession of globally destructive nuclear armaments. Neither the 'blocs' nor their bases will be dismantled, except perhaps to a limited cosmetic extent.

Both in theory and practice, there have to be alternative supra-national sanctions to those provided by nuclear weapons if there is to be real nuclear disarmament; and there are none. Nor do I believe that any will be created.

Morever, conventional wars — and other forms of lesser and non-violent conflict between and within nations — will continue to coexist, and be compatible, with the existence of huge nuclear arsenals for mass destruction, and with the ever-present risk of their use. Indeed it is likely that every kind of instrumentality, both nuclear and non-nuclear, for conducting warfare will continue to be elaborated without cease. Finally, no alternative force for 'national self-defence' can possibly have an equivalent deterrent effect on any 'enemy' to that of nuclear weapons; however fallacious the cybernetic strategic reasoning which underlies the threat to use them.

Therefore, we cannot debate 'alternative' forms of warfare for defence or aggression *in vacuo*, nor set aside — in our heads — weapons of which we morally disapprove, nor conjure up alternative defence proposals out of (very) thin air. That is, we cannot choose between one system of weaponry and another, on grounds of either practical or moral preference, as if such a choice were free. Instead, to avoid illusion, we must reckon first not merely with the permanent human capacity to manufacture nuclear arms, but also with the indefinite perpetuation of their existence, and even with the accelerated proliferation of nuclear bases and weapons — unless or until the weapons are used — since it is the *Realpolitik* of determinate and competing economic and political interests which demands them. The nature of these interests, and of the states whch embody and promote them, will not be transformed or dissolved by the distaste of world public opinion, or even by mass violent protest. Only a world uprising, and the more or less contemporaneous general overthrow of the nuclear states by their citizens on an historically unprecedented scale — an eventuality which I do not believe to be a realistic expectation — could achieve this end.

Secondly, an outbreak of nuclear warfare by accident or design, however 'unthinkable', is a much more likely outcome of the present historical circumstances than either genuine nuclear disarmament or the pacific maintenance of a permanent 'balance of terror'. 'Alternative defence proposals' which discount, by-pass, or pretend by wishful thinking to overcome the irreducible facts of nuclear knowledge, and the political indestructibility (as a likeliest case) of most existing forms of nuclear weaponry, are vitiated at the outset.

Thirdly, even though neither 'national interests' nor 'sovereignty' nor physical safety can, in the last destructive resort, be defended by conventional means — however ingenious — against the use of nuclear weapons, political realism, whether we like it or not, makes its own demands on the advocates of nuclear disarmament.

The main demand is that we grasp, however unwillingly, that a pacifism which turns its back on belligerence is the Achilles heel of the anti-nuclear movement, even if both the logic and the morality of pacifism can be shown to be superior to other logics and other moralities. This will remain the case as long as there are perceived to be — and are — discrete 'national interests' which require 'defending' by 'nation states' on behalf of their ruling classes; an indefinite prospect, which cannot be foreshortened by any degree or kind of disarmament, or by any degree or kind of pacifist intent.

In consequence, the hitherto unacceptable must now be accepted by the Left, both as the lesser of militaristic evils, and as the minimum price — a very high price, but with its own moral claims — of any general public acceptance of a non-nuclear defence policy: namely, reinforced conventional armed forces, and the extension of national service. (A Gandhian moral politics of passive resistance and *satyagraha* cannot be seriously recommended to a British people which has just celebrated 'victory' in the Falklands.)

Moreover, in a world in which a genuine, general and permanent nuclear disarmament will not — and indeed cannot — take place, objection on the part of so many British advocates of a non-nuclear defence policy to all civilian protection against the risks of the use of nuclear weapons cannot be justly or humanely sustained any longer. However ultimately insufficient or imperfect in the outcome, whatever the cost, and however much they allegedly disturb the calculus of the nuclear strategists, the irremovable possibility of future nuclear warfare demands increasing investment in, and the development of, all reasonable protective measures for civilian populations. They are permanently threatened, whether their nations are armed with nuclear weapons or not.

John Shiers: I think that for the foreseeable future we will need professional armed forces for defence against external attack and to aid allies who themselves are under attack. But I think that this should go hand in hand with the development of civilian defence strategies by non-violent direct action. The armed forces need to be transformed from what they are now into organisations of people who see their role as the protection of the political gains made by socialist advances. This means they must be highly politically conscious. Trade-union organisation and accountability in the command structure are vital. So is reducing hierarchy to the minimum necessary to retain efficient organisation and only imposing such discipline as is necessary to function effectively. The socialist values of cooperation and sharing should be explicitly encouraged. Violence, far from being glorified, should be seen as something only to be used in the last resort, after all other strategies have failed. Military hardware must be determined on the basis of its use in stopping an unjust situation rather than its capacity to devastate and destroy the other side.

   A non-nuclear NATO, while we still remain part of the corrupt Western alliance, is clearly a nonsense for socialists. Yet to renounce the possibility of ever having to use armed force against external attack or expansionary aggression from powerful nations who oppose human freedom is to put one's head in the sand. We have to work out policies which take us closer towards where we want to be, but which will answer the worries and anxieties of many people who fear being left 'defenceless' and subject to armed aggression from other nations who oppose us.

Peter Tatchell: The virtues of territorial defence for Britain in the 1980s are persuasive. It gives us the financial, military and moral advantages of pure self-defence in a way which does not require or encourage the use of nuclear weapons — either by ourselves in defence or by our enemies in conquest.

Because it is manifestly defensive and unsuited to external aggression, other countries are unlikely to perceive territorial defence as a threat to their own security. This could encourage them to take similar steps to withdraw from military pacts and the arms race. Territorial defence also increases the possibility of our becoming militarily independent.

In my view, the basis of such a strategy should be territorial defence by a citizens' army.

Being militarily effective and capable of deterring aggression, territorial defence would ensure that Britain could defend itself from attack and invasion, whilst also contributing to the reduction of international tension.

Of a strictly defensive character, territorial defence is not antagonistic to our simultaneous pursuit of détente and disarmament. The sole military objective of territorial defence would be to secure our country's land mass against attack and foreign occupation. It would involve the defence of Britain from within our own borders.

Mobilising the entire population in a system of 'total war', territorial defence would deter invasion by making our country difficult to conquer, with a strategy of harassing and wearing down an invader militarily, through guerrilla war, and also methods of civilian resistance such as strikes, sabotage, boycotts and civil disobedience.

To resist submission to blitzkrieg, or the blackmail of strategic bombing, territorial defence would require the mass provision of civilian protection and the decentralisation and dispersal of key major enemy targets.

Being primarily geared to the prevention of sea-borne invasion and aerial attack, territorial defence would be based on overtly defensive weapon systems such as coastal mines, surface-to-air missiles, interceptor aircraft and anti-tank guns.

These defensive systems are remarkably cost-effective by comparison to the huge capital outlay required for the offensive weaponry on which our present military strategy is based — namely nuclear-warhead intercontinental ballistic missiles, long-range strategic bombers and submarines such as Trident which alone will cost £10,000 million. Relying on the people in arms, territorial defence would require us to move away from dependence on a regular professional army and towards the creation of a genuine citizens' army. This raises the thorny question of universal military service. Being opposed to conscription, I believe a citizens' army should be created out of a radical reform of the Territorial Army to make it attractive for both men and women to enlist voluntarily.

This would probably have to include a statutory right to time off work to attend the initial basic training and periodic refresher courses; plus payment equivalent to a volunteer's ordinary salary.

By basing our defence primarily on our own efforts, it would be quite realistic for us to eventually withdraw from NATO and formulate a foreign policy independent of the United States.

This self-reliance afforded by territorial defence must ultimately be more dependable than a 'nuclear umbrella' controlled by the Pentagon. After all, we have no guarantee that if the crunch came, the Americans would risk the nuclear extermination of their cities for the sake of an increasingly independent-minded Western Europe which has refused to toe the White House line on boycotting the Moscow Olympics and trade sanctions against the Russians.

The defence of democracy requires a democratic system of defence. The defence of world peace requires nuclear disarmament now. Territorial defence by a citizens' army is an alternative non-nuclear defence strategy which could make both these requirements a possibility.

David Taylor: This is another difficult question to answer. I can imagine a lot of sterile argument arising, not out of differences in principle but those of timing. What one might advocate as a policy for 1983 is very different from an ideal policy which one might hope to achieve in ten or twenty years. It is impossible to look at Britain's defence policies in isolation; for example the introduction of non-violent resistance tomorrow without preparation and in isolation would certainly have little deterrent effect, however desirable it might seem to be. My ideal is to achieve the most progressive and far reaching disarmament proposals available at any one time. The first priority must therefore be that of nuclear disarmament. Another high priority would be a programme of education into the techniques of non-violent resistance. All the options suggested in the question are an improvement on the present situation and could therefore be supported, but one cannot go any further without knowing all the other variable factors which might make one policy or another feasible. Ultimately, of course, one would look to a time and a situation when organised non-violent resistance was the only acceptable means of defence — anywhere in the world.

Dafydd Elis Thomas: It seems to me that the key to the reduction of the use of armed force by states relies on the internationalising of relationships between states to the extent that inter-state aggression is responded to on an international basis. I believe the next essential step in international relations is to internationalise the use of force. This has already taken place in a number of attempts at containing situations of inter-state conflict with the use of United Nations troops. What is required is a procedure for rapid deployment of reactive policing by the UN. For internal security, as it is called, a standing army of some kind seems to be the practice of all states, though there would be a 'democratic' argument for the restoration of a citizens' militia.

David Widgery: Assuming (a big if) that a hostile armed force wished to reassert physical control rather than just annihilate the entire island as some sort of 'warning shot' en route to Armageddon, then the only line of effective defence is an armed, trained and united civil population. Mass resistance at the pit-head, the primary school and police station is only going to succeed if there is also a machine-gun under a good many pillows too. Abolition of standing armies and arms for the workers are demands that go back for centuries but would still make the UK an exceedingly unprofitable and difficult island to subdue. Even the tiny guerrilla armies of the nationalists in the six counties and the Basque country have proved highly effective against sophisticated but politically unpopular forces. The best models for this sort of armed popular resistance in periods of revolutionary democracy are the early years of the Soviet republic, Spain in 1936 and Hungary in 1956. But better soon come.

6 What immediate steps could be taken in the direction of the policy you favour?

Frank Allaun: As indicated, the immediate steps should be to end nuclear weapons and to reduce our conventional forces. Although I have no love for either the NATO or Warsaw Pact forces, I am not pressing — certainly at present — that we should leave NATO. Here again I think we must go only so far as the people are prepared to go. They have moved enormously in the last three years, so that CND is today a popular body and getting rid of nuclear weapons is widely accepted. On NATO, however, public opinion polls show that there is a majority in support of it. Similarly in the Labour and trade-union movement there is an overwhelming support for ending nuclear weapons, but only a minority support for getting out of NATO. It is essential that leaders should be one step ahead of the mass of the people, but not ten steps ahead. If they go beyond what a considerable section of the people are prepared to accept, they risk being cut off, isolated and destroyed.

As regards the two steps mentioned above concerning nuclear and non-nuclear weapons, which are our immediate tasks, they can best be achieved by obtaining 1) a Labour government, 2) with those two steps unambiguously stated in its election manifesto, and 3) with the determination to carry them out. This will mean maintaining and increasing the pressure through the trade unions and the constituency Labour parties on the existing leadership. It is essential for these reasons that Michael Foot, who accepts and advocates this policy, should be retained as leader of the party.

Pat Arrowsmith: I'm a member of the Labour party — a fairly recent joiner. Now the party has a more strongly unilateralist position — compared with the 1960s — I think people in CND need to be in it as it's the only party at all likely to form a government that might implement this policy. But of course I don't think joining the Labour party is the only way. We must build in industry and the trade unions — build towards getting effective industrial action against the Bomb. And build in the armed forces. And have peace camps and take direct action. One kind of activity can back up another — they don't cancel each other out or contradict each other.

Meg Beresford: Unilateral nuclear disarmament by Britain as the first step towards the creation of a Nuclear-Free Zone in Europe.

April Carter: Nuclear disarmament by Britain, a 'no first use of nuclear weapons' commitment by NATO, a defence review of British and NATO strategy and armaments, and an official British investigation of non-violent resistance as one element in a defence policy (which some European governments have already sponsored). In the slightly longer term the goal is to move all nuclear weapons out of Europe; a switch to a more clearly defensive conventional strategy in Europe, and attempts to reach agreements with the Soviet Union on forms of conventional arms limitation and disarmament. Preventing a build-up of chemical weapons and seeking agreement on them is also a priority.

Stuart Christie: 'First catch your hare' (Mrs Beeton). The first step would be to democratise the army by introducing military syndicates within the armed services, establish a mechanism whereby these syndicates are coordinated through Soldiers' Councils which would have full power to manage and coordinate the various regiments, corps and establishments as well as taking responsibility for military discipline and counter-intelligence functions.

It would also be essential to ensure both tiers of the defence force were kept independent and separate. Armed defence, for example, should come under the control of a local authority such as the Community Council on which local organisations such as the trades councils etc. were represented. Each local authority would run its own recruitment and training programme and be responsible for its own equipment and back-up services.

Robert Fyson: Get rid of nuclear weapons now and concentrate the attention of the defence establishment on the conventional alternatives. The details of this are for specialists to suggest — I am not one.

Carole Harwood: Firstly the acceptance of personal responsibility, combined with a global perception and psychological transcendence of both existing conditions and traditional perceptions. As the present capitalist system increasingly betrays symptoms of an approaching ideological defeat, its internal polarisations become sharper and more extreme, demanding swifter and more urgent responses from the forces of opposition. Therefore every new imposition of oppression has to be rejected; cruise missiles must not be sited, new anti-gay laws must be actively disobeyed, 'growth' must be obstructed. 'Obstructionism' coupled with a positive optimism could be employed to dismantle the present structure of society wholly geared to the process of accumulation.

We need a new view. A perception of possibilities uninhibited by 'fears' of 'idealism'. Utopianism would no longer be a term of abuse as people, 'Left' as well as 'Right', came to reject the capitalist concept of a work-orientated, profit-dominated mode of existing, where individuals are embarrassed by tenderness and collectivities consider it 'unsound'. Then, perhaps, the 'Left' would cease to take cover in the comforting slogans of 19th century industrial 'socialism' and begin to think in terms of 20th century realities, however unpalatable. The 'Right', in its turn, could then begin to think.

In effect one would work ceaselessly to alter the old mentality of confrontation and to replace it with a developing and flexible hegemonic peace. Christ changed the world, so can we.

Ronald Higgins: Immediate steps in this direction would be the cancellation of Trident, the incorporation of Britain's Polaris fleet in the START negotiations, the postponement (at least) of the final dual-track NATO decision on cruise and Pershing II and fundamental discussions with NATO allies and the Soviet Union on the withdrawal of Forward Based Nuclear Systems from Western and Eastern Europe.

Mary Kaldor: The question here is whether one pursues an alternative defence policy from inside or outside NATO, and I'm increasingly of the view that it's better to do it within NATO. The reasons are twofold. One is that if you look at non-aligned countries such as Sweden, Switzerland, Yugoslavia, they are assuming the continuation of the East-West conflict. They are arming against the possibility of a war in Europe over which they have no control, and in fact they are primary targets in such a war. Many assessments of the military balance say what matters is who gets onto the non-aligned territory first. So pre-emptive invasion is a very high possibility. So in fact they do have to arm themselves to quite a considerable extent, these countries. In our case, because of our fortunate geographical position, I don't think we would have to arm ourselves quite so much. I also don't accept the argument many of the Right put forward that it would be expensive. I think it would be a lot cheaper than our present policy. But I do think it would involve a certain militarisation of British society which I regard as unacceptable. So that's the first reason.

   The second (though again this could be argued) is that we could have a greater influence on the whole East-West conflict by remaining in NATO. I think there are arguments against that and I'm not completely sure; but I think that if we were to stay in NATO and be absolutely uncompromising about trying to shift NATO policy as a whole towards a non-nuclear defensive conventional strategy of the kind I have described (and I think we could use our collective roles in NATO as bargaining tools for that), that could have a more profound influence on denuclearisation than just our getting out of NATO. We could stop cruise and Pershing, we could remove battlefield nuclear weapons from Germany, for instance, and we could use our connections with other social-democrat parties to really build up pressure. At the same time, I think we would have to be pursuing a policy of what I call 'détente from below' with Eastern Europe, so that the whole idea would be a withering away of the blocs and not just defence.

Conditional membership of NATO is my line at the moment. The conditionality doesn't relate to membership but to our collective roles. We say that adhering to the NATO treaty only means that we believe in supporting each other's way of life — more or less. It doesn't say anything. I think what we should say is that we do think it's important to continue this collective security, but we can't allow our forces to be integrated into a military command structure that is based on nuclear strategy. Our two main roles in NATO are the defence of the Atlantic and the British Army of the Rhine. So we'd say, 'We'll keep the British Army of the Rhine provided that battlefield nuclear weapons are removed, cruise and Pershing are not deployed, and there is a step-by-step commitment to the withdrawal of all nuclear weapons over a certain time period.' And in the Atlantic, where we cooperate with the Dutch, we'd say to our Dutch partners, 'Look, we can only go on with this provided that we both remove nuclear depth charges.' We are supposed to give reinforcements to Norway in times of crisis. We'd say, 'We'll give reinforcements to Norway provided Norway becomes part of a Nordic Nuclear-Free Zone.' And I think we'd give NATO between two and three years — shorter than the life of a government, and longer than the planning cycle of NATO — to do this. So that's my policy.

Stephen Maxwell: I favour a 'step-by-step' unilateralism aimed at the eventual disengagement of the United Kingdom from all military alliances.

The first step would be the unconditional renunciation by the United Kingdom of the use, possession or storage of nuclear weapons. This would involve the cancellation of the Trident programme and the discontinuation of the Polaris system.

The second step would be an instruction to the United States to withdraw all nuclear weapons and bases from British territory within a fixed period.

The timing of the third step — British withdrawal from its military alliances — would be determined by the international response to the first two initiatives. It would have three elements:

1) diplomatic initiatives designed to persuade the United States and Soviet Union — and their allies — that the system of military blocs could not survive the indefinite continuation of an arms race between the two superpowers;
2) the announcement of a phased withdrawal of British forces from military alliances;
3) the active sponsorship of proposals for the de-nuclearisation under international guarantee of key areas of the European theatre.

Joan Maynard: It's particularly important for the peace movement to broaden its base and reach out to the working class. We need to get over to people that war has never solved anything.

Jonathan Moore: Due to the radical nature of the changes in the defence structure outlined previously, immediate steps can only be of a particularly limited nature, though in the long term if any real measure of reform is to be achieved these steps must be taken.

Firstly — and perhaps most important — is the need for education and information. It is essential to understand the nature of a problem before seeking solutions; in this case education is needed on the role of the military in Britain, its nature, function and structure, even basic military principles and concepts. Britain seems characterised by a lack of military knowledge amongst the population as a whole. Even to the extent of such basic information as the size, organisation and function of Britain's armed forces. Until this problem of education can begin to be dealt with, then any success in presenting alternatives will be limited. The present situation is, without doubt, a result of policy by government and the services to remove the debate on defence policy away from the public arena. Only in a general campaign of education led by all concerned groups inside Parliament, and particularly by those outside, such as in schools and universities, can much of the uninformed opinion about these issues be combatted and the strengths, weaknesses and nature of alternatives be presented to the public. Indeed, as Suntzu said: 'War is a matter of vital importance to the state; the province of life or death; the road to survival or ruin. It is mandatory that it be thoroughly studied'.[1]

Secondly — a general widening of the debate on defence throughout the country from purely the cruise missile and Trident issues. Lacking the understandably high emotional content of these topics, and so harder to sustain, it is essential that the question of alternative defence policies becomes a major topic of public debate and pressure. To an extent where, even if completely successful on the cruise/Trident issues, the demand for a reappraisal and reform of the 'conventional' defence organisations continues. The strength of the nuclear disarmament case must rest on rational alternative defence policies. In this context political parties at both ends of the spectrum should make a serious and determined attempt to analyse their position as far as non-nuclear defence is concerned, and formulate constructive policies to be presented to a hopefully more informed public, and electorate.

1   Suntzu, *The Art of War*, translated by Samuel B Griffith (Oxford, 1963), p 63.

Thirdly — arising directly from the above points — there should be developed a campaign from political parties, interested groups and the public in general for the establishment of some form of voluntary militia, open to all, and initially with the sole purpose of the defence of Britain's home territory. In the context of the present threat envisaged from the Soviet Union, it could provide a useful counter to *Desant* and diversionary forces and possibly release Regular forces and reserves for Germany. At the same time it would show that many people are committed to defence of the nation, without having to defend the nation 'full-time' by joining the Regulars or field reserve, the Territorial Army. A problem which since Haldane's reform has always faced the concerned citizen.

What would be essential is that such a force be trained, organised, recruited and commanded completely separately from the Regular forces, at least initially, to avoid the negative values inherent in Regular forces such as careerism, class consciousness and anti-intellect values. It would be controlled directly by Parliament with commanders recruited from within the organisation itself and definitely not from the existing officer corps or from retired army personnel, for reasons above. An age limit of perhaps 35-40 could be placed on membership.

An institution of this nature would provide a starting-point for further reform: in fact rather than be seen as a new feature it is a return to England's traditional militia forces. Any opposition to such a proposal, of which there would be a great deal, would serve the beneficial function of highlighting the question surrounding Britain's defence structures and how they could be changed. And, most importantly, why certain specific groups in Britain were opposing a genuine attempt by citizens to assist in the defence of the nation, and whose interests are really being served in opposing such an organisation.

However, in the short term, it is difficult to see any real change in policy, and long-term radical reform is unlikely unless part and parcel of a widespread movement emphasising new political and social goals — this is a crux of the educational programme.

Ann Pettit: Plainly we are seeing the beginnings of the end for militarism. First we must outlaw the use of military force for purposes aggressive rather than defensive. Then we must start a 'swords into ploughshares' process with our arms industry. In fact, if the nuclear threat is ever sufficiently averted, the emphasis of the international movement as a whole could well shift over to striking at the business and arms trade link-ups. The Falklands war at least brought clearly home to many people that the weapons of the world all go round in big circles. Underlying this is the whole question of 'sovereign states' — the 'bits' of the world we 'defend'. How far have we progressed towards agreement over who-has-what-bit? Well, there's Ireland and Israel, where people are still locked in bitter dispute over who-lives-where and who-gets-to-decide. In other words, these disputes are not so much 'sovereign state' quarrels as disputes between groups of people about justice, and this includes most of the other regions of the world where wars are going on. Overlaid on basic disputes about justice, and land, are the powerful nations manipulating groups to ensure that whatever the outcome of a conflict in local terms, they hang on to what they want — be it the oil, the uranium, or the possibility of a 'friendly' country where military bases can be constructed.

Now in the end, we are going to see a militarisation of the whole world, and space as well, if we do not begin to outlaw and render obsolete the very idea of military 'defence' as having any purpose that is not ultimately anti-social. We have done this in many countries within the communities — except in the USA, which is still in the antiquated position of equating 'freedom' with the freedom of everybody to possess sophisticated means of killing. But in most countries it is no longer considered right and proper to simply have a shoot-out with your neighbour if his teenage kids wake you up at all hours, or if he has cheated you. So maybe what we have to do, in the long term, is extend our ideas about 'civilised' behaviour to cover relations between what are called 'states'.

Chris Savory: With a policy of organised non-violent resistance it is essential to build up the strategy while we still have a military defence. The initiative needs to be taken by disarmament/peace groups and 'nuclear-free' local authorities in putting on educational and training programmes for people. Schools could disband cadet corps and start non-violent training instead. Unions could take the ideas of non-violent defence to the workplace. The widespread adoption of non-violent direct action tactics by the peace movement is an important step towards developing an effective non-violent defence.

David Selbourne: First, the fact that there is now such little moral restraint on the limit of what is considered 'thinkable' in the strategic and tactical use of nuclear weapons, itself licences those who are opposed to such weapons to think — both creatively and destructively — beyond their present inhibitions about morally acceptable counter-measures. Although such an outcome is unlikely, it would arguably be just if protest were to proceed, beyond peaceful demonstration, to other forms of individual and collective physical intervention against the further technical development, transportation and emplacement of nuclear weapons, in order to give the fullest expression to citizen fear and outrage.

Secondly, though the momentum of all such physical protest — hitherto largely middle-class — against nuclear missile and bomb emplacements may in fact not be maintained, domestic public debate in Britain about *all* issues relating to defence and defence expenditure must be increasingly joined by the Left. (This will probably prove to be closer to the maximum outcome of the current offensive against nuclear weapons than any genuine nuclear disarmament, whether in Britain or anywhere else.) But in order for the reach of its positions to be as wide as possible, its demands for the unilateral abandonment of nuclear weapons in Britain, and for general nuclear-arms reduction, must immediately be clearly distinguished in the public mind from pacifism, if the failure of its campaign is not to be hastened.

Thus the British Left should now take the national initiative in calling for the extension of national service by conscription, and for the maintenance — and even increase — of existing levels of expenditure on the modernisation of Britain's conventional forces. It must also demand a large-scale programme of national public works to protect the people, as far as is economically and politically possible, against the consequences of deliberate or accidental nuclear attack.

Unless it adopts such policies as these — which is highly improbable — it will lose the political battle genuinely to divest Britain of its nuclear weapons and bases even more decisively than already seems likely.

John Shiers:

i) The immediate unilateral renunciation of all nuclear weapons.

ii) Hand in hand with this the development of a European non-nuclear defence strategy, in common with socialist movements in other parts of Europe. The basic principles to be withdrawal from the NATO alliance and an independent foreign and defence policy non-aligned with either the USA or the USSR.

iii) Trade-union organisation in the armed forces; the replacement of all existing military leadership; a new emphasis on political education; collective non-hierarchical organisation and accountability. Women to be admitted as equal members at every level.

iv) Training in non-violent resistance and civilian defence for every person in the society as part of education. The integration of this training with political consciousness-raising throughout the society.

David Taylor: Many of us will be tempted to propose immediate steps which are more radical than the political situation will allow. We need to remember that we can only advocate, for immediate enactment, those policies which have a chance of gaining general support. We are therefore unlikely to see any disarmament initiatives in the short term; the most we can expect is to stop any further escalation, and cancellation of cruise and Trident for example. Further steps will require more education, so that when these policies are enacted, they can carry a majority of people with them.

As soon as it's politically feasible, we should close all foreign bases and take Britain out of NATO. We should adopt a position of positive neutralism between the USA and the USSR and urge other European states, on both sides of the Iron Curtain, to join us in building a broadly based non-aligned movement. A stance of positive European neutrality would deny the military forces of both superpowers access to Europe and act as a psychological and physical buffer zone between them.

In the meantime there is much that we can do to develop a programme of non-violence training through-out society — in pressure groups, local government and the workplace. Trade unions already organise strikes and pickets. What about some blockades, boycotts and fasts? Without waiting for government action we could introduce non-violent direct action (NVDA) training to churches, schools and social clubs. Was there ever a better way of getting to know people?

David Widgery: How (and if) we can get the vast distance from present-day UK reality to such a society requires another twenty pages. The 'immediate step' one takes in that direction is to try and translate one's imagination of that possible future of the cosmos down to the small chips of life and struggle as it exists in Thatcherite Britain. While fiercely retaining the larger vision. Which might mean an inquorate union meeting which can none-the-less hold people together, or a protest picket line which changes a few minds, or organising a coach to

Greenham Common. In my case, today, it involved failing to sell a copy of *Socialist Worker* to someone who thought Tadworth Hospital should be closed. But having a first-rate argument with them. As for the abolition of the officer army, the re-direction of the pro-digious technology of the arms industry into socially useful directions, women's admirable lack of enthusiasm for the armed forces and their role in a real peace corps, there are plenty of suggestions and directions already. But (and dissenting from the views of the editors of this volume) there is very little point in drawing up detailed blueprints until we have convinced more of our fellow-citizens of the argument that there is a more secure, productive and practical basis on which to organise society than along the priorities offered by Mrs Thatcher's Warfare State (and the undistinguished attempt at Welfare Capitalism that preceded it). This means reinstating a vision of socialism which is both hard-headed and soft-hearted, which can express and utilise the creative abilities and human sensibilities which are at present frustrated and embittered. It does not mean pretending we can get rid of the Bomb and somehow leave the present pattern of life in Totnes and Blackheath and NW5 unaltered. Not comic opera Bolshevism but action and argument which shows how immoral, unrepresentative, ineffective and potentially self-immolating the system based on the remorseless accumulation of capital has become. And how we, the people, and our needs and our abilities can provide an alternative and an end to its crazy logic.

The important thing to cultivate now is what Brecht called the art of thinking inside other people's heads. For, in the words of the famous Trotsky quote which Walter Benjamin first used and then deleted from the manuscript of *The Author as Producer;* 'When enlightened pacifists undertake to abolish war by means of rationalist arguments, they are simply ridiculous. When the armed masses start to take up the arguments of Reason against War, however, this signifies the end of war.'

7 Do you see any other country as offering a model for an alternative defence policy in Britain?

Frank Allaun: There are many countries which are clearly ahead of the British government in their defence policies. I refer first of all to Canada. In 1978 Mr Trudeau told the UN special conference on disarmament that henceforth the Canadian air force would not carry nuclear weapons either on the American or European continents. He has kept that promise. Admittedly Canada has a smaller population than Britain, but strategically it is a very important country. Norway and Denmark will not have nuclear weapons or nuclear preparations on their own territory in time of peace. Greece has joined NATO but refuses nuclear weapons. Belgium, Holland and, most important, West Germany, are all preparing to refuse the cruise missiles, or certainly their Labour parties are. I am not suggesting that they are an ideal model for an alternative defence policy, but they are certainly ahead of the policies of Mrs Thatcher's government. All these countries are at present in NATO.

Pat Arrowsmith: Well of course there's India and Gandhi, and things that happened in the United States in the civil rights movement. Part of the Hungarian uprising was non-violent, and there's Poland and Solidarity today. Czechoslovakia in 1968 wasn't a model of success, but if taken a bit further the kind of non-violent resistance they took there might possibly have achieved its purpose. Perhaps that's pie in the sky, but we don't really know because there has never yet been a country that has actually, as national policy, decided to adopt a non-violent defence policy; though some years ago the Swedish government did initiate some research into non-violent resistance — not from a principled position, but because it might be effective. The possibility of this happening is, I think, demonstrated by resistance movements within a country. If you get massive movements against nuclear weapons, or against, say, racial discrimination, which manage to achieve their objectives through non-violent resistance, then this can demonstrate that such a tactic could be viable nationally.

April Carter: For a non-aligned Britain, Sweden perhaps comes closest to offering a model for a defensive military policy. Costa Rica is the only example I know of a country which abandoned armed forces, because the internal threat they posed seemed greater than the military threat from its neighbours, and is not at all comparable with Britain, though an important case study.

Stuart Christie: Not really. There are certainly some useful lessons to be drawn from the experiences of such countries as Switzerland, Israel, Yugoslavia and so on, but there are more important historical models such as the Makhnovist Insurrectionary Army of the Ukraine in revolutionary Russia which was organised along libertarian principles. There are also later examples such as the popular militias organised by the labour unions in Spain during the Civil War, Durruti's Iron Column and the Madrid-based National Council of Defence. More importantly, in the British context, there is Tom Wintringham's invaluable contribution to the subject of democratic defence policies and the experiences of the Local Defence Volunteers, inspired by the Spanish popular militias. Wintringham's ideas and experiences would certainly be worthwhile re-examining in the light of modern-day requirements.

Robert Fyson: No, not precisely, though we can learn something by studying the defence policies of all the non-nuclear-armed European states.

Carole Harwood: No.

Ronald Higgins: No single country could offer a complete model but we could learn something from Sweden's posture of defensive deterrence (including its willingness to pay more per capita for defence than we do). There are however important differences. They have a tradition of neutrality: we do not. Note that Swedish security in practice depends considerably on NATO's existence. A Europe of Swedens would be much more vulnerable to Soviet pressure than Europe is now.

Mary Kaldor: No. I just don't think that the non-aligned countries are relevant.

Stephen Maxwell: The Swedish and Swiss policies of armed neutrality, aimed first at minimising the risk of becoming involved in war, and second at deterring an invasion by demonstrating the military capacity to exact a price disproportionate to any advantage the aggressor could hope for, offer the best models.

Joan Maynard: I suppose any countries that employ a non-nuclear strategy, such as Sweden, Switzerland or Yugoslavia.

Chris Savory: At the moment there is no country that has developed a sophisticated programme of non-violent defence. However, other countries are also investigating the possibilities of non-nuclear defence and they might take a lead in this. For example, 'social defence' is an important part of Die Grünen's peace programme in Germany.

David Selbourne: No other country — and certainly not Sweden, nor Switzerland — presents a like constellation of historical, political, economic and military characteristics to those of Britain. They include a large and increasing nuclear armoury, American military occupation, a substantial defence industry, a history of global imperialism, an archaic structure of political and economic institutions, a continuing war in Northern Ireland, and an essentially reactionary trade union movement — both at the bureaucratic and rank-and-file levels — with little interest in nuclear disarmament or national defence policy.

An alternative defence policy for Britain must therefore meet the specific case of Britain. Neither a foreign 'model', nor a set of universal utopian prescriptions — in particular if they discount the nature and temper of British nationalism — can possibly do this.

John Shiers: Not in its entirety; but I think we can learn something from the organisation of the armed forces and civil defence in Sweden, Norway and other Scandinavian societies.

Peter Tatchell: Although a strategy of territorial defence by a citizens' army may be a startling departure from conventional British military wisdom, it has been the long-standing cornerstone of European countries as diverse as Yugoslavia, Switzerland and the Scandinavian social-democracies. Utilising territorial defence, these small countries have been able to preserve their sovereignty from the ambitions of great powers. Without nuclear weapons, Belgrade was able to avoid the fate of Prague. Further afield, using the techniques of 'in depth' guerrilla war, a country as small and poor as Vietnam was able to humiliate the mightiest military machine on earth.

Even in our own recent British history, the Home Guard of the 1939-45 war represents a precedent for teritorial defence. At its peak, the Home Guard consisted of 1.5 million members, largely organised into workplace units to defend the shipyards, mines, railways and factories in the event of Nazi invasion.

David Taylor: The pressure of the arms race, economic competition and international tension are such that every country feels itself obliged to have some form of military protection. Even those countries that have adopted a neutralist stance, such as Switzerland and Yugoslavia, find themselves obliged to maintain a conscripted national army. If Britain adopted a neutralist position, there would undoubtedly be pressure from those over here who want to re-introduce conscription.

8   Questions of defence cannot be separated ultimately from wider questions of international relations. What principles should govern British foreign policy in future?

Frank Allaun: As regards foreign policy, I greatly prefer the Swedish government to the present British government. Sweden has constantly attacked the division of the world between the rich North and the poor South. It has encouraged democratic action in other countries. It has opened its doors to refugees from tyrannical regimes in many parts of the world. British foreign policy should not involve fighting wars in other countries. That is not to say it should not encourage non-violent democratic movements under attack or suppression by dictatorial governments, whether in Chile, El Salvador, Namibia or Turkey.

Pat Arrowsmith: I think British foreign policy has to be considered in relation to our membership of NATO, which can't be seen apart from the capitalist implications of being part of the Western alliance or from the implications of being neutral vis-à-vis the Warsaw Pact. I'm a socialist. I don't wish to be part of American capitalism and all that's implicit in NATO. And that leads on to the business of being in the EEC and so on. I don't want Britain to be part of capitalist alliances. Similarly, I wouldn't want Britain to be part of the Warsaw alliance. It's a military alliance: it relies on nuclear weapons and it's debatable how far it's a socialist alliance anyway — depending on how you define socialism. I wouldn't think it was. Consequently I believe this country should be very actively neutral. It should be neutral in the sense that it shouldn't be part of the alliances, just as Finland, Austria, Yugoslavia, Switzerland and Sweden are not. But it should not merely opt out. Those countries have not had any nuclear weapons; they haven't been prominent in an alliance in the way Britain in a sense has. But were we to get out of the alliance we're in, I would hope and think this might be quite significant and might lead to a toppling of that whole alliance and what it stands for. So were we to leave NATO, this might lead to a quite different kind of foreign policy in Europe and the world — at least I would like to think so, though I'm not sure if Britain is as important as all that.

Meg Beresford: British foreign policy should be based on a realistic view of our position in the world. We have to recognise that we are a small, relatively unimportant offshore European island. We should take our part in rectifying the North-South inequalities highlighted by the Brandt report, and we should take the environmental and ecological threats to the planet into account in our foreign relations. We should take steps to rectify the serious inequalities in our own society — for example, 36 per cent of all the cases taken to the European Court of Human Rights are from Britain. We should make responsible use of international agencies for solving problems.

April Carter: This question requires a separate book. Very briefly: active promotion of all forms of disarmament, starting with nuclear-free zones; strengthening the UN and its peace-keeping role; seeking an end to the division of Europe into military blocs; trying to limit and control the arms trade; serious commitment to economic development in the South (how this should best be pursued is a huge question in itself).

Stuart Christie: International policy should be directed towards encouraging a libertarian alternative to statism and multinational consumer capitalism that is not marxism-leninism. The peoples of Africa, Asia, Latin America and the Middle East should be given solidarity in throwing off the tutelage of multinational capitalism which views the world as its factory, farm and supermarket and, in order to secure its investment, imposes and bolsters the most repressive and barbaric regimes imaginable. The net result of this policy is to throw the developing countries into the hands of one or other of the two Eastern bloc countries.

Robert Fyson: Cut loose from subservience to American global strategic, political and economic perspectives. Pursue an independent non-aligned approach, within the context of the community of European states. Work to change the EEC rather than leaving it — all European socialists and liberals want us to stay in.

Carole Harwood: For a start let's have some 'international relations'! By this I don't mean the highly structured, highly paid elitist ritual we call diplomacy, in fact I mean quite the reverse. Instead of the sidelong suspicious manoeuvrings of governments conscious of their 'investments', let's expand the existing channels of alternative communications. An international peace movement exists, why not use this avenue in the pursuit of 'security' rather than officials committed to the conflict/profit ethic?

It would be useful to begin at the beginning by recognising our exploitative past and our present duty to the Third World. Not in terms of charitable aid, but starting with a self-imposed vision of global realities as viewed from the comfort of a rich metropolitan country. Only by a wholesale redistribution of resources can all the inhabitants of our Earth ever begin to approach some sort of equality. Without obstructing 'growth' in the developed world there can be no realistic possibility of the Third World tackling the problem of starvation genocide. The conscience of the bloated Northern axis can no longer be salved by pouring Nestle's multinational milk into the pot bellies of aid/relief programmes. We know the water to mix the profitable milk powder kills. We know we use millions of gallons of water to machine-wash our cheap clothes from Taiwan. Until we comprehend what these connections means there can be no 'international relations', only a one-sided subsidy of starvation on the one hand and a continued and destructive drive towards expansion on the other. How about the principles of humanity governing British foreign policy in future, after all it hasn't been tried so far and look at the mess to date?

Ronald Higgins: British foreign policy should respond to global realities both East-West and North-South. In practice we have been parochial, cautiously self-centred and absurdly short-sighted. Various global threats including population increase, resource shortage, environmental degradation and nuclear proliferation as described in my book *The Seventh Enemy* have been converging fast, and the still widening poverty gap between North and South cries out for the kind of 'programme for survival' urged in the Brandt reports.

We need therefore to construe our 'national interests' in a radically enlarged and long-term fashion. Nor is this over-ambitious. We are still a rich, powerful, influential and stable nation, and the only one that is at once a member of the EEC, OECD, NATO, the Common-wealth and the UN Security Council.

Mary Kaldor: I do think that the most important thing is to overcome the confrontation between East and West, and that should be the fundamental principle that governs our policy. And this means that it governs our attitude to NATO and it governs our attitude to the Third World — that we're always trying to support progressive forces in the Third World and to give them space between the blocs. We must utterly oppose military blocs of any kind.

Stephen Maxwell: As a neutral country the United Kingdom could expect to have only a modest role in international affairs. The general objectives of its policy should be:
1) to contribute to the creation of an international environment sympathetic to arms control and disarmament efforts;

2) to support reform of the international economic system in favour of the countries of the Third World;
3) to give political and material support to national liberation movements and diplomatic support to civil rights campaigners;
4) to strengthen those international institutions which advance the cause of a fairer distribution of the world's resources.

Joan Maynard: Well I think the top priority should be détente. We should try to get nations to work together, not build up arms. And our economic policies should also be devoted towards that. The more countries that are really socialist, the less likelihood of war. War is an extension of politics. Capitalism is an aggressive form of society, it encourages aggression. We have to get over to people that if they cooperate for the good of the majority we will have a good society. Concrete example is much better than talk here.

Chris Savory: If Britain is to disarm and play a constructive role in world affairs, we must cease to operate a neo-colonial economic system which stops healthy relations with the developing world. In general, British foreign policy must be governed by an understanding of our aggressive imperial past, with the realisation that peoples should not seek to dominate and subjugate others. Of immediate political concern is the need to break down the cold war barriers. This necessitates the creation of a strong non-aligned force in world politics, which Britain should be a part of. So international cooperation and positive internationalism must be guiding principles of British foreign policy. A great deal more honesty, openness and a sense of morality must enter our international relations.

David Selbourne: If foreign policy were, or were to become, a matter of free choices — it isn't, and won't — determined by the light of reason and moral principle alone, very little of Britain's foreign policy, Tory or

Labour, would be defensible. (Most of it is not in our longer-term political or economic interests either.)

Thus in Erewhon, or a similar utopia, we would abandon our dreams of national grandeur along with our 'independent deterrent', resign our place on the board of NATO, and end our gross complicity in world-wide structures of industrial and financial exploitation of post-colonial and other dependent nations.

We would also act upon the reports of Amnesty International; uphold the principles of the UN charter and the Universal Declaration of Human Rights in our own internal affairs and foreign relations; withdraw militarily from Northern Ireland and politico-econo-mically from South Africa; replace 'development aid' (and the fiction of the 'Commonwealth') with genuinely needed forms of mutual collaboration; and give all assistance, military, political and economic, to the struggles against neo-colonialism in Latin America, Africa and Asia.

The minimum precondition for such a change of direction in British foreign policy — beyond the cosmetic — would be a domestic political revolution. In its absence we will continue, essentially, to do what we are doing, come hell or high water.

John Shiers: The task for socialists in the West must be to convince the majority of people that all our lives would be better if we ceased to exploit and live off the backs of other nations. I doubt whether this will be done by the traditional Marxist means of arguing that socialism is about more material goodies for all of us in the West. It is more likely to happen by increasing numbers of people seeing that without redistribution of wealth on an international basis we aren't going to have a world much longer for any of us to live in. Unchecked industrial expansion in pursuit of more and more material goods for our consumption will destroy the Earth's ecological balance in the end. The business of holding on to the wealth we have gained already by our manipulation of power is going to become increasingly hard as poor nations collectively organise. Competing with the Soviet Union for control over the Earth's resources will mean our mutual destruction. These are the realities which we have to present to people, however unpalatable they seem.

David Taylor: The nation-state mentality, like the party-political mentality, can be divisive and dangerous. It glorifies the self-image of a nation by devaluing that of others. Its self-centredness doesn't recognise that what is good for the whole is also good for its parts. In the age of microchip communication and space travel we urgently need to see ourselves, not as a collection of bickering nations, but as one world. It is this internationalist vision that must underlie any British foreign policy. This will mean completely re-thinking our global economic strategy, at present geared almost solely towards the short-term material advantage of a minority of the world's population in the industrialised North. Cashing in on finite resources, ripping up the Amazon jungle, rationalising EEC agriculture, central-ising production and discharging radioactive waste into the sea — these are all short-sighted and dangerous ideas. The same mentality that gives us these short-term policies also gives us an inward-looking nationalistic perspective, and the latter-day empires — the super-power blocs.

An international economic policy designed to increase international stability would emphasise the need to cut out waste, put back into the Earth that which we take out and generally work towards the principle of self-sufficiency. In other words produce as much as possible locally. Think globally and act locally! Not only does it make sense in strict defence terms to be less reliant on other parts of the world, it also creates a diversity of tasks within any one community and thereby nourishes the local culture and identity. This principle should apply throughout the world. How much Third World land that should be growing food for local consumption is in fact being used to grow cash crops to line the pockets of a small minority of landowners?

Central to all traditional political parties is the notion of economic growth. Growth needs an ever-increasing supply of energy and raw materials, material resources which are finite. As consumption increases and raw materials become more difficult to obtain, prices rise — hence inflation. Competition becomes fiercer and tension is heightened. Resource competition has been a central factor in many wars and will be so again — economic growth is fundamentally unstable. We are now rapidly approaching a situation in which governments will feel obliged by the domestic heat of their consumer societies to take ever more extreme measures to maintain their supplies. This is the main factor which led the USA to set up a Rapid Deployment Force. The key word in all of this is 'sustainability'. Tension cannot be lessened unless we begin to develop a sustainable economic order.

In addition to economic competition for the betterment of any one class or nation, the nation-state mentality plays another gruesome role in the suppression of minority groups and native peoples — known as the Fourth World. The centralisation of social structures and economic planning has badly damaged many minority cultures.

Dafydd Elis Thomas: British foreign policy should in the first instance be anti-imperialist. This means that it should no longer be part of aggressive alliances, or undertake its own military actions such as the Malvinas/Falklands war. Its first adherence should be to a much strengthened United Nations Organisation; economic and cultural policy should seek to actively promote more equitable relations between North and South as being a positive contribution to maintaining international law and order through reducing economic differentials.

David Widgery: Foreign policy is all very well. But if it's all you've got then it doesn't matter how brilliant it is. Once Babylon is smashed a sensible policy for Great Britain would be to wind up at once all its colonies and colonial outposts, change its name to the Revolutionary Federation of North-West European Islands and (if our Irish neighbours are of like mind) move its capital to Dublin. From whence a historic popular assembly of the free men and women of England, Scotland, Ireland and Wales would declare that the Federation's principal concern is that people live on the planet together, productively, cooperatively and without trying to impose their beliefs on others, repudiate our imperial and colonial pasts and announce that our green and pleasant land would be from now on devoted to equi-sexual and multi-racial democracy, productive and useful labour, care of the weak, modest cultivation of appropriate fuel and food, life-long universal education (including life-long target practice) and the greater creative glory of the language, the music and the landscape. Our foreign policy would be to convince the rulers of the rest of the unenlightened world that we had better be left alone to get on with it. And, more importantly, convincing the workers of the rest of the world of the necessity of following our example. But convince, not seek to impose by force, from above.

9 **The present character of the British armed forces is strongly marked by Britain's history of imperialism and class division. How might a programme of military reform tackle the internal organisation of the armed forces, and how would this depend on other social advances?**

Frank Allaun: I am quite certain that the answer to this question is to form and encourage trade unions in the armed forces. This would be the best way to answer the class divisions within those forces. In almost every country the military officers, particularly in the top ranks, are the most reactionary caste in society. It is quite wrong to allow them to have the uncontrolled power over their men which is certainly not tolerated inside British industry.

In many European countries such as Holland and West Germany trade unions exist and flourish, even in certain cases for officers. Clearly they are not allowed to disobey instructions during a war, but they do have a great deal to do, and say about conditions in the forces. Such matters as wages, hours, training and working conditions are constantly under negotiation. Most important, to my mind, is that they provide a strong safeguard against fascist tendencies or dictatorial attitudes amongst the officer class.

In Britain it is permitted for certain small categories to continue membership of the respective unions to which they belonged in their previous civilian life. What is now required is permission for trade-union organisers to meet the men and women in their canteens and elsewhere, to explain to them the advantages of joining a union, telling them of what happens in other countries, and collecting their subscriptions. No doubt if these unions eventually became associated with other unions it would disincline the servicemen to be used as strike-breakers in the event of industrial disputes in Britain. That would be a good thing.

Pat Arrowsmith: It's a difficult question for a pacifist who doesn't believe in armed forces anyway. However, I'm quite aware, from my commitment to the Troops Out [of Ireland] Movement, that the British armed forces are indoctrinated to assume that the nationalist people in Ireland are the 'niggers' and to discriminate against them. I've met people who've been in the army in Ireland and heard about how they've been indoctrinated. I hope the British armed forces may become more like some of the other armies of the world with soldiers, sailors and air force people objecting to reliance on nuclear strategy. If you get armed forces whose members are against using nuclear weapons, this can be very subversive. My CND group passed a resolution that those workers most directly responsible for nuclear war strategies, namely the armed forces, should be encouraged to form CND groups. This sort of thing has been happenning recently in Europe — in Germany and Holland. It would be very encouraging and helpful were it to happen in this country. We mustn't forget the part played by disaffected GIs in ending the Vietnam war.

April Carter: I don't know how to alter the character of the British armed forces effectively. Conscription would not necessarily affect the regular forces significantly — it doesn't seem to have in the post-war period — although of course highly politicised conscripts might press for internal changes, a soldiers' trade union, etc. as in Holland. It might help to change their role, and so attract rather different people: for example specially trained UN contingents, even more emphasis on air-sea rescue and a social service role for the forces. But I suspect that changes in society and in the social groups now recruited into the forces may be essential.

Stuart Christie: According to the *Guardian* (16 October 1980) at least 50 per cent of the officer class has been recruited from public schools, but I seriously doubt if a policy of wider recruitment would change the nature of the officer corps. In the USA, for example, the officer corps is, on the whole, representative of the community as a whole — but it doesn't improve it any! Officers represent a superior class and, even if they don't come from it, they are there to ensure the loyalty of the army to the established order. Officers perceive themselves as 'professional people' (i.e. those whose education and upbringing lead them to believe they are the natural and impartial administrators of society), but in effect their 'officer quality' rating is assessed on their ability to get others to obey them. Those sort of attitudes and relationships are anachronistic and have no place in a genuinely democratic defence force. Ranks should be limited to sergeant, corporal, etc., and reflect accumulated experience of dealing with people, military expertise and, above all, the confidence of those with whom they live and work. The officer corps as such should be abolished and the technical, scientific, logistical and managerial functions normally assumed to be the domain of officers and the Ministry of Defence would be taken over by other specialist corps subject to the same rules and regulations as the rest of the defence force and not exercising political or military control over it.

There has been no military intervention in the political life of this country since Cromwell, nor has militarism ever been a strong force in British politics, but the danger with any army in any state is that if you give it power to deal with external or internal enemies, ultimately it will rule the country. The main trend in contemporary military thinking is towards the internal rather than the external threat. The growing obsession with the threat of organised labour as a tool of Soviet subversion and counter-insurgency has greatly increased the politicisation of British army officers. With the impinging friendship circles of their class in industry, banking and political life, this makes a potentially dangerous enemy which feels threatened and sensitive to any move seen as likely to diminish or weaken its ability to defend itself. In effect, any radical re-structuring of the armed forces would have to follow a major scandal such as a failed 'pre-emptive' coup or evidence of major corruption or malfeasance.

Robert Fyson: I don't altogether accept the assumptions of the question. I have no direct experience, or specialist knowledge, of the British armed forces, but I believe they are now much less dominated by rigid class stratification than in the past, and much more meritocratic in character. No doubt there is room for improvement, but reforming their internal organisation does not seem to me an urgent priority in the context of the main issue — i.e. the preservation of human life on this planet.

Carole Harwood: Britain's history of class division and imperialism is certainly reinforced by the presence of an army, elite or otherwise. Arguments about 'revolutionary' armies don't seem to substantially alter the argument. Such armies do certainly behave in a democratic/heroic/revolutionary way, but only at particular moments within a precise historical context. Sometimes prior to that moment, and indisputably subsequent to it, such an army inevitably reverts to its militaristic character. It was, after all, revolutionary armies that executed the Levellers in the 17th century, the enragés in the 18th, the workers of the 1848 June Days in the 19th and the sailors of Kronstadt in the 20th centuries. The appropriation of a revolution by the military is a contradiction to be avoided.

As to how 'a programme of military reform' could tackle the internal organisation of the armed forces, I suspect it couldn't — and shouldn't. I don't want a more liberal, democratic and effective army; I don't want an army at all.

Ronald Higgins: Britain's armed forces are not strongly marked by 'imperialism'. There may be residues of racism, just as there are in the trade unions. In general however our soldiers are probably happier defending the independence of black Belize than the privileges of White Anglo-Saxon Protestantism in Northern Ireland.

The armed forces are marked by class division, if less so as the years pass. This is both bad and silly: it must reduce effectiveness.

This said, it is hardly a prime duty of the armed services to reform Britain's social structure. If we want that done *we* must do it.

Mary Kaldor: One proposal for reform that comes up quite often is that we ought to have trade unions in the armed forces and that the armed forces should be run much more democratically — say, with the election of officers. I can see the advantages of that, actually, from the point of view of the problems of command, which I believe are very great now. When war becomes hideous, it becomes much more difficult to ensure that people obey what you say. And the traditional forms of command — loyalty, patriotism and so on — are very arcane, and though they do still exist in the British armed forces, it's rather unusual and it's very much out of keeping with the times. And it might be that a much more democratic way of organising the armed forces would be much more effective militarily. But again, that brings me back to the problem, do we actually want to create armed forces that are more effective militarily? So I'm very perplexed about this. My own inclination is to say let things be; strengthen parliamentary and civilian controls over the military, rather than tackle any real major reforms.

Stephen Maxwell: It is a redeeming feature of Britain that despite its imperial past and the more recent glorification of military values in the Falklands conflict, its professional military elites have not made — let alone established — any claim to political leadership. The political influence which the military enjoys in Britain derives rather from its place in the class structure of

British society and, more important, from its status as an
entrenched 'interest' in the state bureaucracy. Unilateral
nuclear disarmament, the withdrawal from military
alliances and such other steps as the replacement of the
professional army by a citizens' militia, will help to
'demystify' the profession of arms and reduce the
general prestige of the military. The class base of the
military elite will be weakened only by egalitarian social
and educational reforms. The power the military enjoys
as an entrenched bureaucratic interest is just one aspect
of the wider problem of the accountability of state
power, to be solved (only with great difficulty) through
radical reforms of the political system and the state
apparatus.

Joan Maynard: This depends on political advance towards
a more progressive society. There should be trade unions
in the armed forces so that people can express their point
of view. The unquestioning loyalty demanded of people
who join the armed forces doesn't appeal to me — loyalty
to the present society and to their superiors. A more
democratic army would in the end be a much stronger
fighting force. But this could only come from a more
progressive society. I'm a great supporter of open government, freedom of information. Most important decisions
now are taken behind the backs of Parliament and even
the Cabinet — certainly behind the backs of the people.

Jonathan Moore: This question has been dealt with to
some degree by my previous answers. Military reform —
that is of a politically entrenched powerful national
structure — is only possible when (1) a demand for
reform from the external political executive is met by (2)
pressure for reform from a strong reformist group
within the military structure and the people in general.
When such alliance or harmony of interest is found,
there is real possibility of genuine change in purpose
which develops into functional and structural reform.
Such a situation existed in Prussia from 1801-1813 and
was successful. Similar genuine reform changes

occurred in France due to revolution. This has never been the case in England.

Reformers in military organisations usually are found at colonel level — such people, however, do not form a power group and external political reformers do not move so low in the rank structure as to come into contact with them. Like all organisations, the military resist change bitterly, and in the case of Britain they have been usually very successful, particularly in dealing with attempts to reform its purpose.

It is the question of *purpose* which is paramount in understanding the problems of instituting a reform programme. In the case of the British military, its purposes have been threefold:

1) Internal security. The protection of the state from internal threat.
2) Dynastic and imperial expansion with the later purpose of an Empire police force.
3) National defence.

From this purpose, the function and structures developed. In the case of Britain a small, regular, 'volunteer' army, cloistered from society. Thereupon it develops a system of cultural, social and political values divorced generally from the society it is supposed to serve. This encourages the outlook that the army retains the true 'virtues' of the state, at a time when such 'traditional' values are being 'undermined'. Such an attitude naturally increases the organisation's conservative nature and any attempted reform is seen as a direct attack on the values of the 'nation'.

The adoption of this purpose has been to establish the military as a supporting pillar of the state, providing it with the final argument against internal opposition. The continuous and close identification of interest between military and state which has existed since the Restoration enables the army to take a passive role in the political arena, while remaining an instrument of direct political action. The first problem any attempt at implementing a reform programme faces, is that any attempt at reform of purpose threatens not just the structure and attitudes within the armed forces but the vested interests of particular groups in society. Thus any real reform of the military purpose becomes impossible without actual political and constitutional change. Usually such reform occurs after a catastrophic defeat or revolution, where the interests of ruling groups are discredited or overthrown. British reformers have all failed to overcome the problem.

Many attempts have been made at reforming the structures and functions of the armed forces. The military reforms of Cardwell and Haldane both tackled various problems successfully. However, the nature of their reforms was limited by the fact that they did not challenge the actual validity of the military system, in terms of its then ostensible purpose — the defence of the nation. What they achieved was to alter specific aspects of structure, making them more efficient in terms of their existing function, but little else. Any programme of internal reform will founder on this problem, that is if it hopes to achieve more than merely tinkering with the system. As in the case of Prussia, major change in structure and function is dependent on a change in purpose.

It must be stressed that any change in purpose (from, for example, internal security to national defence) which attempts to carry out this purpose by using existing military structures, will result in the corruption of the whole system by the transfer of values, attitudes, approaches and perceived roles from existing structures into the new, leading to dysfunction on a massive scale. It was in this fashion that the Home Guard in the Second World War, a genuine popular attempt at a new military organism, was captured by the army, resulting in the Home Guard becoming a part-time replica of the Regular army.

An attempt at military reform must in effect develop completely new purpose, structures and functions. Only the reform of the basic purpose of a military system can lead to real functional and structural changes. Ultimately it is the purpose for which a military system is designed which defines its character and nature. This enabled the British army to withstand the two great periods of conscription without endangering the organism. Although the structure rapidly expanded, a dichotomy was preserved between the Regular and the 'duration' elements. De-mobilisation merely resulted in a contraction in structure leaving the Regular system relatively undisturbed. As for radical reformers, they were dealt with in traditional fashion: internal radical reformers are purged completely, or posted into harmless areas: certainly such individuals will be considered as 'quite a bit mad'.[1] An external threat is pushed into fringe areas of political activity, the reformers dismissed as 'traitors' or 'subversive'.

A programme for real reform, as outlined earlier, that is a radical alteration in purpose, can only come through external political action linked to demands for reform. The interconnecting nature of political, social and military institutions makes military reform dependent on the engine of social and political change. However, as my previous answers show, military reform in Britain is only likely to arise by the creation of military organisations — controlled by democratic institutions — from outside the existing Regular forces.

Chris Savory: The gradual disbanding of the armed forces will obviously be a very delicate process. However, ordinary servicemen (and women) are not totally isolated from the 'outside' world, and would themselves be responding to the changes in society. Many would be more than willing to leave the services if society could provide meaningful work and a decent living standard for them. Without widespread social change it is inconceivable that the power of the military could be seriously undermined.

---

1   General Sir Henry Pownall describing Orde Wingate. *Chief of Staff. The Diaries of Sir Henry Pownall*, Volume II, (London, 1974), p 126. Edited by B Bonds.

David Selbourne: The internal organisation of the armed forces would begin to change — though to a marginal degree of democratisation only, short of a more general political revolution — under the restoration of national service by conscription. (This is an additional reason for espousing it, particularly in a period of the army's brutalisation as a result of the war in Northern Ireland, and of the recruitment of lumpen unemployed from Britain's industrial wastelands.

But no means now exist, without the entirely unlikely overthrow of the state apparatus itself, to bring the police or the armed forces under more than superficial political control, let alone direct democratic accountability to the community. The nature and form of the electronic technologies, and the weapon and information systems, which are increasingly at their disposal, together with the elite and anonymous organisational structures which accompany them, can now neither be publicly scrutinised nor democratically reformed. They can only be physically destroyed.

And the paradox is that they will not be physically destroyed, except in a nuclear holocaust.

John Shiers: The dependence of all this on other social advances is obviously key. Everything I have written presupposes a commitment from the majority of people in England, Wales and Scotland towards a fundamentally different route from the one we are presently travelling along. The task for socialists is to make this case in a way which relates to most people's actual experiences in their society. This involves providing detailed answers to the real fears and anxieties people have that radical change may make things worse for them. Yet today there are several new areas of struggle and forms of resistance growing outside the workplace, as challenges to the international capitalist order. The peace movement, the ecological movement, the women's liberation movement and the gay movement are all about power which is not simply a reflection of ownership of wealth. They all emphasise, too, the quality of life around us and call for new ways of being which will, I think, become increasingly appealing. All is not well in the West as its capitalist economies lurch from crisis to crisis, and mass unemployment becomes a permanent feature of the new technological capitalism. If the creative forces unleashed by these movements can fuse with the existing class forces represented by the traditional Labour movement in a new alliance for change, then I think hope remains.

Peter Tatchell: It would necessitate a long overdue democratisation of the armed forces. This would include abolition of petty regulations, relaxation of harsh military discipline and the extension of full civil, political and trade-union rights to soldiers along the lines of the Dutch, Norwegian and Swedish armies. Whilst British service personnel cannot actively participate in political parties or trade unions, or even write to their MP without the authorisation of their commanding officer, military reforms in Sweden have already advanced to the stage of 'co-determination' between officers and lower ranks.

David Taylor: Of all our economic and social institutions, it is the army and navy that most trenchantly maintain class division. Straight from public school, the 'officer and gentleman' will understand little about the men and women under his command. The first step towards a more collective and less hierarchically based system would be the introduction of elections for all posts within the military. This will be a painful process initially, as both ranks are so used to the existence of an 'officer and gentleman' class.

The armed services are divorced from the communities in which they were formerly based not just because recruitment tends to be spread more widely over the country but also because of the way in which the military organise themselves. Imagine the effect — on anyone — of a uniform and military haircut together with separate accommodation, training and courts! One vital form of democratisation would simply be to integrate the military more closely into the local community. A specialised and separate unit can be an immunised unit, immunised from the feelings, understandings and goals of the civilian population — and that can be very dangerous.

At present the armed services are usually in the rearguard of social advance; just look at their attitudes towards homosexuality, class and race. The internal organisation of the armed forces is in urgent need of reform, if for nothing else then simply to keep pace with social advances being made in other spheres. The reactionary attitudes of many officers are derived from their education at public schools. Such schools are very often divorced from their communities and earn their reputation by encouraging competition and militarism. As public-school children are taught to lead, so are state-school children taught to be led. Educational reform must therefore go hand in hand with military reform, with public-school reform being high on the list of priorities!

Dafydd Elis Thomas: The first requirement of military reform is the unionisation of the armed forces and the replacement of hierarchical structures by a far more democratic structure of internal and external accountability. This would clearly be resisted by those who would wish to maintain traditional notions of 'discipline', but the disciplines of collaboration are different, rather than less, than the discipline of hierarchical pecking orders. Such democratisation of the standing army, navy and air force could only be successful as part of a more popular movement of democratisation.

10 Military coups are a relatively common experience in countries beset by political and economic crises. The British army now devotes a great deal of energy to counter-insurgency training, i.e. against internal 'threats to national security'. Do you see any danger of the army being used to thwart the will of the people? If so, how should democrats act to prevent this?

Frank Allaun: During the last war the educational services inside the forces did a valuable job in preparing men for a return to civilian life, and for the kind of social and political changes which post-war Britain would need. Today I suspect that these ideals have gone through the window, and that the indoctrination of servicemen takes place by extremely reactionary officers in many cases.

The suggestion of using the army against internal 'threats to national security' is I think rather remote at the moment, if those words imply a revolutionary threat. However, servicemen have been used on a number of occasions since 1945 against other working men. If Mrs Thatcher received a second term of government I suspect that the army might be used more often in such circumstances. The best safeguard is the development of trade-unionism among the servicemen themselves — that is, of course, apart from having a more democratic government in Westminster.

I think a far greater danger is the influence of the top brass of the forces being used to thwart moves to end nuclear weapons and for conventional arms cuts. This is depicted very strikingly in the novel *A Very British Coup* by Chris Mullin. I suspect that several of the chiefs of staff used their influence for sending a task force to the Falklands. I have also witnessed myself the participation of these brass-hats against CND and its policies. Here again, nearly everything depends on having a government of determined democrats in power.

There may be a suggestion of election of the top officers. This would be a desirable thing, but I see little hope of it occurring for a long time ahead. The more immediate step is for the setting up of trade unions in the forces. There must in addition be constant disclosure of reactionary moves in the future. The book by Brigadier Kitson reveals the kind of mentality which needs exposure.

Pat Arrowsmith: In Britain, it's quite plain that the army is being used for counter-insurgency — and not only in Northern Ireland but in England and Scotland too. It's been used in the firefighters' strike and in the refuse collectors' strike in Scotland. That is perhaps one of the reasons for opposing the whole notion of having an army. Armies can be used in this way. They're not unbiased: they're not just 'peacekeepers' with an unprejudiced position — they're used by the government of the day. And the government of the day in Britain is a capitalist government, aligned with the bosses in our society and not with the ordinary people.

I spoke in a 'This house would not fight for queen and country' debate in the Cambridge Union a couple of years ago, and Field-Marshal Carver was one of the other speakers. In the course of the debate I questioned him about a coup that was brewing in the armed forces at the time of the miners' strike in 1974. And he equivocated, but he in effect admitted that there were various signs in the armed forces suggesting that people were thinking about a coup. To be very gloomy, if we elect a Labour government committed to unilateralism, one asks oneself, will this be implemented? Are the powers that be going to see that the policy is carried out? Are the Americans going to permit it? One only has to look at Irish history to see how the army can revolt against government policy — I mean the Curragh mutiny against the Home Rule policy of the English government. And this could happen again. One way to guard against the danger of a unilateralist policy not being carried out is to build support for CND in the armed forces.

Meg Beresford: Yes. The signs are that the army will be used against perceived internal threats to national security. We should work towards the abolition of official secrecy and for a genuinely open form of decision making, as well as for the disbandment of special army and police squads like the SAS and the SPG which are specially trained for counter-insurgency.

April Carter: Yes, it is quite conceivable the army might be used to crush certain movements or to back up some kind of political coup (I don't see a direct military coup occurring) though it does not seem a high probability. How we should respond must depend on the circumstances, but basically by strikes, civil disobedience, non-cooperation and whatever forms of non-violent resistance seem appropriate and possible.

Stuart Christie: Pio Baroja once said about the (Spanish) army: 'In times of peace it shoots the people. In times of war it runs away.' A more contemporary observer, Field-Marshal Lord Carver, wrote in his prefatory endorsement of General Sir Frank Kitson's *Low Intensity Operations:* 'If a genuine and serious grievance arose, such as might result from a significant drop in the standard of living, all those who dissipate their protest over a wide variety of causes might concentrate their efforts and produce a situation which was beyond the power of the police to handle. Should this happen, the army would be required to restore the position rapidly. Fumbling at this juncture might have grave consequences, even to the extent of undermining confidence in the whole system of government.' The fact is that if people are sufficiently motivated to take to the streets, occupy factories and take over the public services, then it is unlikely that the government will have the confidence of the people. One should also ask, to what position is it the army would restore us?

The possibility of the British army 'thwarting the will' of the people of this country certainly exists, but I doubt if it would follow the Chilean or Greek models. The British officer class are traditionalist and conservative enough to realise that any military intervention in the political life of the country would have to take into account British political traditions and the strength of the organised labour movement as well as an anti-militarist public opinion. I think that the experience of the British army in Northern Ireland has taught it its own basic limitations in internal security. If there was a coup in this country I think it would be more along the lines of the Gaullist coup of 1958. The only way democrats can actually prevent such a thing happening is by ensuring the armed and security services are answerable and responsive to the wishes and needs of the people as a whole. We should also remind ourselves that it is ourselves alone, not soldiers, policemen or civil servants, who are ultimately responsible for safeguarding our lives and 'national security'. Our freedom and our hopes for a better world are far too precious to be left in the hands of policemen and soldiers.

Robert Fyson: It is right to be eternally vigilant, but British army counter-insurgency training is mainly aimed, I think, at terrorism by e.g. the IRA, for which I have no sympathy. I don't think armed insurgency in Britain is likely, or would be *popular*, i.e. supported by the majority. The army is not big enough to take over the country, and there is no tradition of army involvement in British politics. The threats posed by the 'security state' to our liberties are real and insidious, but more subtle than a direct military coup. To suppose that the events in Chile in 1973 are likely to be re-enacted here against a socialist government seems to me pure fantasy. I am worried about what the army would be ordered to do in the aftermath of nuclear war, but if nuclear war occurs all is lost in any case.

Carole Harwood: After 44 women were arrested for dancing and singing on the silos at Greenham Common air base, we were eventually locked up in locker-sized, double-fastened steel-fronted cages. There was just enough room for one person, but because of our numbers some women were packed two together during the long motorway journey to various police stations. I was outraged that we should be treated like terrorists, until it struck me with a considerable chill of fear that, in real terms, we were. By opposing the development and advocating the abolition of the arms race we were putting in jeopardy probably the most massive financial deals ever, deals involving the most corrupt, powerful and irresponsible functionaries of capital. In this sense the threat the peace movement poses is much greater to governments than that, say, of the Red Brigades, because we are not playing by their rules, we don't dip into the same arsenal. In this sense, then, the state apparatus is already aimed at our foreheads; a fact we should confront with calm and determination. We should embrace total non-cooperation at every level, including the industrial and domestic, and reject fear. Indeed it is fear which often creates political impotence, particularly fear of our own government, our own army. By translating this fear into a creative realisation that while we are essentially 'in opposition' we can only function effectively if we actively oppose, we can then face the oppression of the state machinery confident of its weakness and our own strength.

Mary Kaldor: Yes, I really do see a danger of the army being used to thwart the people. I don't see there being a regular military coup in this country; a lot of people talked about that in the early seventies. I just don't think that's how things happen — but that doesn't mean to say that I don't see a situation in which the army is used more and more for things like strike-breaking, breaking up demonstrations — certainly if we get more violence. I could see those kinds of developments occurring. And those, I think, are very worrying and very frightening.

And again I don't know what the answer to that is, except that we should be tremendously vigilant, and demand all sorts of citizens' rights, and demand that the army should not be used for these purposes, and try to introduce various forms of parliamentary control.

Ronald Higgins: The British army is bound to devote some energy to counter-insurgency training. Guerrilla action and terrorism figure substantially in Northern Ireland. They did in the Confrontation War in Eastern Malaysia. They could well do so in a European war.

There must of course be some danger of these capacities being abused if anything like civil war were to emerge in Britain. But, if it did, some military counter-action might be justified. (What if the 'insurgents' were armed racists?) In any case I am impressed by the firmly democratic and constitutionalist attitude of most of the senior military people I meet.

Stephen Maxwell: The danger of the British military intervening to prevent a properly elected government from adopting radically new security policies is small, and could be made smaller by reforms of the electoral system to ensure a more truly *representative* legislature. There is no tradition of military intervention in modern British politics and there are many alternative centres of political mobilisation. Nuclear disarmers and neutralists should, however, publicise the possibility of military intervention, and through their trade union and political contacts prepare contingency plans for what, in a complex modern state, would be the most effective response — a general strike.

Joan Maynard: I do see it as a danger. It's very much linked up with what's going on in Ireland. I happen to be very interested in the Irish question. The British working class is making a great mistake not to press for a political solution to the Irish question. We have repression there by both parliamentary and military means. You can't deny freedom to others and keep it yourself. The Prevention of Terrorism Act is a threat to our own civil liberties, people can be arrested and held under that Act for seven days without charge. In fact most of the people arrested under the Prevention of Terrorism Act have never been charged, in the end just released. If the army is training for counter-insurgency, this is designed to meet difficulties that might face them in mainland Britain. It's another argument for democratising the army and bringing it closer to the people. That's not easy, because all our institutions are there to uphold the present society which they're part of.

Chris Savory: If there is the possibility of real social change in Britain that is against the interests of the government and the ruling class, it is definitely conceivable that the armed services will be used to thwart change. For example, if the peace movement gets strong enough to really challenge the power of the state, and there is widespread industrial action or non-violent direct action that actually succeeds in, say, closing down a military base, the government will be faced with two choices. 1) To support the wishes of the people. 2) To use the armed services to try and crush the wishes of the people.

I still believe enough in the idea of British democracy to feel that a military takeover of the government is unlikely. However, if a unilateralist, anti-NATO government was elected in Britain, I would not dismiss the possibility of the US trying to put pressure on that government by stirring up and supporting opposition in Britain's military.

In order to work against the power of the military, people need to 1) create a non-violent force that cannot be crushed; 2) constantly expose publicly the possible threats that the military poses to our civil liberties and democracy; 3) influence ordinary servicemen and women and try to get them to think about what they are doing.

David Selbourne: The army, particularly in Northern Ireland, is *already* used to 'thwart the will of the people'. Its involvement, for instance, in domestic political surveillance and information gathering of all kinds throughout Britain is already substantial, and growing. Democrats — to say nothing of successive Labour governments — have already failed to prevent it.

An overt military coup d'état is less necessary, the closer the already well-established and largely hidden nexus becomes between the police, the army, the mandarinate of the Ministry of Defence and the intelligence services, and the inner circle of Cabinet committees. None of this apparatus is democratically accountable, and most of it is unknown to the electorate.

The British political system is already one of dual power: that of the secret state, on the one hand, and of parliamentarism and other liberal-democratic forms on the other. In such circumstances, and however the political and economic condition of the country worsens, a coup d'état ought not to be needed.

John Shiers: The armed forces would obviously present a major danger to any movement for progressive change which came near to gaining power in Britain. It is frightening how little the Labour left have thought through how to deal with this threat and that the first real contribution to the debate has been Chris Mullin's novel *A Very British Coup*. I think the majority of the leadership of the Labour left feel, as Tony Benn appears to, that the military would not do such a thing in Britain if a left Labour government had a genuine mandate from the people.

Socialists must speak about the realities of the way in which, in one society after another, the armed forces of the state have defended the interests of those who hold power and wealth within it. We must not seek power through a coup d'état or a minority government. Rather we should base our tactics on the need to build a broad alliance between a whole number of groups whose interests converge in seeing the need to dismantle the existing state and the interests which it represents. We can also make a start now, in training ourselves in non-violent direct action techniques and restoring the sense that socialism is a movement which is about the quality of our lives and all our social relations, not just about who holds state power.

Peter Tatchell: The civilianisation and democratisation of the armed forces entailed by a mass citizens' army and smaller professional forces could be an important means of facilitating greater democratic control and accountability of military power. It would certainly lessen the possibility that the armed forces could ever seize power in a coup or be used as an instrument of strike-breaking and civil repression by a right-wing government.

David Taylor: Yes, I think there is a real threat. The army and navy are the bulwark of reaction in this country. Not only do they traditionally adopt conservative attitudes, they are also less inclined towards democracy than many other professions. The army and navy are not exactly known for democracy themselves! 'If it works well here, why shouldn't the country be run along the same lines?', one might imagine them saying. A coup d'état seems a long way off, but military intervention in industrial disputes is already accepted — e.g. the fire brigades, ambulance drivers and refuse workers. The best preventive approach would be the establishment of a genuinely decentralised democracy that took away much of the power of central government and integrated the armed forces more closely into the community. Military elections with full officer accountability would probably be the single most effective means of preventing a coup d'état.

Dafydd Elis Thomas: The kind of popular movement of democratisation across the board which I referred to earlier would seem to me to be the most critically effective way of preventing a right-wing coup from thwarting electorally endorsed popular demands. A clear necessity is the deepening of consciousness of democratic rights through participatory procedures and understanding developed through far more substantial political education of the fragile basis of democracy itself. The only effective means of defending democracy is through extending its practice.

11 **It is widely recognised that defence policy is significantly influenced by the arms industries — whether private or state-owned. In Britain the manufacture and sale of armaments provides employment and exports. How would you deal with the 'defence industries' and the arms trade?**

Frank Allaun: The sale of arms is a dirty business. The excuse normally given is, 'Well, if we don't sell arms, then other countries will.' That is the excuse of the drug pusher, an excuse which is not accepted in a court of law, or from a moral standpoint.

It is undoubted that the sale of arms has encouraged hostilities between other countries, as well as providing reactionary governments with weapons against their own peoples.

Certainly the private manufacture of armaments is particularly disgusting: that directors and shareholders should make profits from endangering the spilling of blood of people in other countries is intolerable. Whilst I am in favour of public ownership of the arms industries for many reasons, principally to take the profit out of arms sales, nevertheless one must admit that the state-owned arms industries in Britain seem almost as keen on selling their weapons abroad as the private armaments manufacturers.

The Defence Sales Organisation is part of the Defence Ministry. It employs 400 staff, many of them skilled engineers. Instead of flogging sophisticated planes, tanks and other weapons to desperately poor countries throughout the world, the DSO should be closed down and the 400 staff switched to the sale of civilian engineering goods to other countries. Floating exhibitions of armaments on British ships should be ended, as should the annual arms exhibitions in England for foreign dealers.

The more serious argument for such manufacture and sales is that they provide jobs. It has been shown beyond doubt that £1 million invested in the arms industries provides fewer jobs than £1 million invested in civilian manufactures. If we were not wasting £15 billion a year on 'defence', we could be using that money to provide jobs in building, education, the health service, re-equipping industry and aid to the hungry nations.

It is vital that we do not face British workers with the alternative of arms jobs or unemployment. Whilst a large number would be employed in the peaceful services mentioned above, nevertheless there are a number of highly skilled engineers who might lose their jobs. It is essential that their specialised skills and their highly sophisticated factories should be engaged in equally skilled work of a non-military kind. Lucas Aerospace shop stewards national committee, re-presenting twelve Lucas factories, devised a 1200-page plan for alternative peaceful work for their members. It proposed such things as kidney machines and other advanced medical equipment, vehicles which could travel equally well by road or on rail, vehicles which travel partially on petrol and partially on batteries, harnessing the energy provided by wind, water and sun, heat pumps for warming houses at a lower cost, and many other valuable things. Several of these have been adopted by others with success, but the management turned down the corporate plan virtually on the spot. Other shop stewards committees, notably at Vickers and Rolls-Royce, prepared less ambitious proposals, but here again there has been little adoption of the schemes.

An engineer working on a lathe can turn out a small steel cylinder equally suitable for use in a tractor or a tank. Most engineers would infinitely prefer that they were engaged on tractors. They do not have the choice. It is up to the government to ensure that the work is there on non-military projects. If arms spending were cut, the money would be immediately available for providing socially valuable work such as the construct-ion of houses, roads, sewers, improved hospital services and more places at universities and colleges of technology.

Pat Arrowsmith: I think many people in the anti-war movement recognise that the arms industries have a ghastly momentum of their own which probably defines policies, in the United States as well as in this country. The truth is that countries which are not investing too much of their personpower, their research and development, and their manufacturing potential in arms industries are much more prosperous than us — Japan for instance — whether they're capitalist or not. The arms industry is very unstable and it's capital- not labour-intensive, among other things. And working in armaments is also unstable in this country. In the past there were plans to produce the Blue Streak missile and TSR2 bomber, and when they were dropped the people working on these armaments went on the slag heap in the labour market. This question is very pertinent for me at the moment because I'm on London CND Trade Union Committee and we're just about to launch a project at one of the major arms firms in London, up at Enfield — Thorn EMI — raising the issues implied in your question. If you work in the arms industry your job is unstable, but conversion is possible — there are plenty of examples to show that conversion to non-armaments production is feasible. But even if it's not instantly feasible, an economy where so much is devoted to arms manufacture is not a profitable economy — and this is clear from the statistics — not just in this country but in the United States too — vis-à-vis Japan and other countries.

I'm not an economist, but I think one or two things are instructive. One is that at the end of World War II, 9 million people, I think, were redeployed from munitions manufacturing into purely civilian production within 12 months. And more recently in the United States there were some interesting cases of firms being converted from military production. In Britain blueprints have been produced by workers at Bristol Aircraft, Lucas and Vickers showing how firms can be converted from military to civilian production. But I doubt really

whether large-scale conversion would be feasible
without a quite different kind of economic policy
altogether, involving a different kind of government
with different priorities. I'm a socialist, so naturally I'm
going to think in those terms.

Meg Beresford: By positive and concerted efforts
towards conversion to socially useful production.

April Carter: I don't really have answers. One important
factor is the kind of arms used for British defence; a
switch from high technology weapons to simpler
military technology would reduce economic pressure to
sell abroad in order to break even, but there would be a
strong demand for simpler and cheaper weapons in
many countries. Trade union and government pressure
on firms to diversify, so they are not too specialised in
arms, might help. International agreement of some kind
on what type of arms should be sold and to whom would
be desirable, but difficult to reach and difficult to
enforce.

Stuart Christie: Our approach to the sale of arms abroad
would have to reflect our foreign policy with regard to
the Third World and developing nations. We would
obviously be obliged to provide arms and weapons
systems to friends in need. The big problem is
identifying what is a genuine need and what is not. It
would be worthwhile taking note of what the workers of
Lucas Aerospace have done in this respect. One
approach would be to ensure only workers' coops were
licensed to manufacture and sell armaments and that the
members of the coops were provided with regular
background briefing on the political, social, military and
religious situation in those countries which placed the
orders. There would also need to be further safeguards
that the arms were in fact for the use of those for whom
they were ostensibly purchased.

Robert Fyson: Conversion of present 'defence industries' surplus to requirements to peaceful uses. Scrap Aldermaston, etc. altogether, and employ scientists to devise means of running down and making safe all present nuclear facilities, civil and military. Stop the export of arms for profit. (Detailed plans exist, though I have no space or expertise to go into detail.)

Carole Harwood: £11 million per minute is spent on arms. It is a growth industry. 'Growth' is essential to the arms race and vice versa.

40 million people die each year of starvation. 'Growth' is the major threat to our eco-survival. The arms race has brought us to the edge of annihilation.

It is no longer useful to confront this sort of equation with slogans like 'jobs not bombs', however well-meaning. If 'no bombs' means 'no jobs', then it must be no jobs and we should be prepared to face the human consequences responsibly.

We have to reject the legitimised paranoia that has made international distrust and fear a political way of life, and replace it with a mentality of cooperation and positive trust between peoples, while negatively accelerating the collapse of the present accumulative rule of capital which collaborates with the foul profiteering of the arms traders in sentencing 12 million children a year to death by starvation. It is impossible to separate the arms trade and the spectre of Third World starvation — both have death in mind, neither can be tolerated.

Ronald Higgins: It is certainly true that the military-industrial complexes have achieved more influence than is desirable, especially perhaps the arms technologists, who constantly devise new systems which the military and especially the politicians find hard to resist.

Here again however easy indignation makes a poor guide. Some arms are necessary; so therefore are some arms industries and designers. The necessary safeguards cannot lie in the total abolition of arms industries and laboratories but in more sensible and firm political direction. This will require far greater sophistication from politicians about security issues and therefore a higher quality of public questioning and pressure.

Formal public control of the private arms industries might help, but the core of the late twentieth-century problem is not a conspiracy amongst capitalist merchants of death; but outmoded thinking about war, 'bargaining from strength' and so on.

As to the arms trade, not least to the Third World, any hope for its restraint will depend on international agreement both East-West and amongst the major Western suppliers. Such agreement is more likely to follow a deepening détente than precede it. Meanwhile Britain should if necessary unilaterally decide to sell arms only to NATO and Commonwealth countries. This is to draw a somewhat arbitrary line, but to decide sales policy on goodie/baddie lines can become unreal, offensive and unduly troublesome. This restraint would of course be expensive in terms of earnings and jobs but you have to start somewhere.

Mary Kaldor: This, for me, is a huge question. Yes, I think defence policy is significantly influenced by the arms industries — in fact I would say that the Cold War is institutionalised in the structure between the arms companies and the government. If we want to change our defence policy, an absolutely essential prerequisite is to change the relationship between arms industries and government. At the moment the arms companies — although most of them now are state-owned — operate as private entities, and are absolutely dependent on orders both from the government and from the arms trade. And that means tremendous pressure builds up for new weapons, which is difficult to withstand. I could go on at length about that. So my view is, I think it's right that arms industries are state-owned but wrong that they're dependent on military orders. And what's going to be absolutely essential is to make it clear to them that a certain minimum capacity for arms is maintained irrespective of whether or not they get new orders, as was traditional in the Royal Ordnance factories, so that they don't feel the pressure always to build new weapons, and that there be a real programme of conversion of the arms industries into other more socially useful purposes, so that their main outlets are socially useful outlets instead of military outlets.

Stephen Maxwell: As an armed neutral Britain would require to meet a significant part of its armaments needs from its own industries. There would be some scope for arms exports, primarily to other neutral or at least non-aligned countries and to some national liberation movements. The problem of surplus capacity in the arms industries is no different from the problem of surplus capacity in other industries, to be solved by a combination of macro-economic policy, investment in alternative industries, retraining and social policy.

Joan Maynard: I would discuss with the trade unions who organise the workers in these industries, and with the workers themselves. We must provide alternative jobs, jobs that are socially useful and not destructive. This has to be tackled head-on.

Chris Savory: Modern industrial society and weapons of mass destruction are inseparable partners. The 'defence' industries and the arms trade are just the most obvious links. The values that underpin an exploitative, dehumanised, violent mode of economic production make modern militarism possible. A change of values will mean rejecting militarism *and* our present system of production.

Enormous power is held by very large corporations, many of which are directly involved in military production. These companies are obviously a powerful block to effective disarmament. No doubt if nuclear disarmament occurs they will be pressing for large conventional forces. So how can their power be countered? First of all, by realising that we need to, and can, change our system of production. The corporations have power now because they can threaten governments and workers with unemployment. To undermine this we have to change our present concept of work, integrating work with the rest of our lives and ensuring that people's material needs are met properly, whether they have a recognised job or not. Other necessary changes would entail greater economic self-sufficiency for Britain, production based as far as possible locally and producing for real *needs*. Big business, like governments, only has power over us because we let them have it. In the industrialised part of the world we exchange material 'goodies' for power over our own lives. Worse than that, through our involvement in the arms trade we help oppress other people. So how do we change? Well, as consumers we have to stop being seduced into over-consumption, and learn to live simply. As producers we have to develop a system of production that follows the guidelines above. In this process, workers in current military industries will play a key role as they develop alternative production strategies and then take control of production. The government will need to use its power to enforce the halting of Britain's part in the arms trade, and will have to exert pressure for other governments to do the same. The government will also have a major role to play in the redistribution of wealth and incomes that will be essential if we are to accept a lower material standard of living.

David Selbourne: The logic of the rejection of, and the resistance to, nuclear weapons is the logic of an increased 'defence industry'; certainly of one that is not diminished. Public ownership could do something — though not much, since it would be locked into the secret state apparatus — to make the defence and arms industry publicly accountable. But short of political revolution, and perhaps not even then, neither its technologies, not its budgets, nor its company accounts, nor its filiations with American and other defence establishments, could or would now be made visible to the public.

The same applies to the possibility of general control over the arms trade, as the record of past Labour governments amply shows.

David Taylor: This is a difficult one. Look for example at the Sandinistas in Nicaragua. I would find it difficult to offer them financial and diplomatic support and then deny them arms, particularly when I believe that we should maintain an armed defence force here at least in the short term. Despite this, the arms trade is grotesque and Britain's record far from blameless. We are, in fact, the world's fourth largest arms-exporting country — thus we have directly contributed to countless wars and many thousands of deaths. We clearly have a historic responsibility to cut back on the arms trade. The industries should be encouraged instead to produce socially useful alternatives. We need only produce those weapons needed by our own military, other non-aligned countries, and oppressed people involved in liberation struggles.

Dafydd Elis Thomas: All arms manufacture should be brought into public ownership run by workers' control at plant level.

12   Do you see a role for protective civil defence in a nuclear-free Britain?

Frank Allaun: I do not see any role for civil defence at present. It would encourage the idea that Britain can be protected against nuclear bombs, which is a complete myth. There is no defence against nuclear war except to prevent it from happening. If twelve 1-megaton bombs were dropped on Britain, the country would become virtually uninhabitable. If they are dropped, I hope that I and my family are under the first one, because then we would die immediately, whereas if we were fifty miles away we would still die — in agony — weeks later, because the atmosphere, soil, water and food would be radioactive. As for the VIPs sheltering five storeys below the surface, they would have to emerge sometime, and what kind of a world would they face? In addition, civil defence involves a large number of people in actually preparing for a third world war. Whilst many of them would be well-intentioned people, there would also be an attraction for some of the more reactionary-minded members of the population to participate.

These same arguments apply, although to a lesser extent, to civil defence after Britain has gone non-nuclear. If we were nuclear-free, it is far less likely that we should suffer a nuclear bombardment. It could be argued there might be some protection against radio-activity arising over Britain from nuclear war in some other country. However, deep shelters would be no use against radioactivity. Again — far from providing the British people with some assurance of defence against attack — civil defence would tend to make them believe it even *more* likely that they would be subjected to attack.

There are now 140 local authorities which have declared themselves nuclear-free zones. This means that they will do their best to refuse to undertake civil defence work imposed on them by the Home Office. It would be contrary to their admirable efforts if civil defence were introduced either before or after Britain went non-nuclear. Or rather the mockery of civil defence, which is largely an illusion.

Pat Arrowsmith: Yes, possibly. That may sound strange, but just possibly. One of the things that is appalling about civil defence in Britain today is that it is part of an aggressive strategy, because if you say that you can defend the country, whether it's by anti-ballistic missiles (which we don't have) or by protecting the population, you're in effect saying that we can afford to wage a nuclear war because we can protect a significant number of our people — which is not what Switzerland and Sweden say. All they're saying is, we don't have anything to do with the main alliances — the nuclear-based alliances — but as we don't want our people to be killed if there were to be a nuclear war, we'll put them underground and try to devise effective shelters for them. They're not taking an aggressive stand by doing this. Anyway it's a complete confidence trick to try to fool the people of Britain, which is plastered with nuclear bases, that they could really be protected in a nuclear war.

Meg Beresford: Yes, if we are genuinely nuclear-free.

April Carter: Yes, in a non-nuclear Britain where some kind of civil defence would become a genuine possibility, I think there is a strong case for some measures to protect people from fallout. Whether an enormously expensive deep shelter programme is realistic or desirable is questionable, but this is an area which a non-nuclear Britain should look at very seriously.

Stuart Christie: I can see no justification at all for sustaining the myth that there is any defence whatsoever against nuclear attack — other than ensuring Britain is declared a nuclear-free zone. On the other hand, however, there may well be a case for some sort of voluntary rescue service capable of responding to local and national disasters.

Lisa Foley: Proponents of civil defence argue that civil defence planning would save considerable numbers of lives during and after nuclear attack. They often attempt to minimise the devastation they expect after nuclear attack and to deceive the public about their chances of survival. They also intend to use the civil defence structure (Regional Seats of Government — the unelected government in reserve for national emergencies) as a way of controlling the populace.

In spite of these drawbacks, civil defence deserves our attention. Any government which took the initiative to denuclearise its forces and set up an alternative defence structure must tear down the old civil defence structure to be used *against* us and set up a much looser, more democratic system to be used *for* us.

Many unilateralists are opposed to civil defence preparations because they judge them by civil defence as we know it now — a total sham. An alternative system is required because it would be irresponsible to allow people to die who could have been saved by some basic education and tools for self-protection. While civil defence may be next to worthless in the case of direct nuclear attack — no matter how alternative it is — it could prove important in other scenarios, e.g. radiation drift from attacks thousands of miles away, conventional bombings, or even from certain types of chemical or biological warfare. In sum, some amount of civil defence would appear to be an essential ingredient of any humane defence policy.

The new civil defence experts must make *realistic* assessments of what amount of radiation is survivable and at what distance; they must as accurately as possible publicise which safety precautions would be worthwhile and also advise the public how to recognise the long-term as well as short-term effects of nuclear attack (such as cancer). The health services should be better equipped to deal with wartime emergencies in a way that would expand their capacities during peacetime.

Once the true limits of civil defence are recognised and made public, it seems there would be no choice but to make some basic preparations to ease the worst damages of a possible future survivable war.

Robert Fyson: Yes, possibly — against fallout from nuclear war elsewhere. No use if Britain were a target.

Carole Harwood: I found this question particularly hard (as opposed to the others which I found very hard!). The temptation is to embrace, once again, the old mentality of fear and distrust; to begin again to prepare for war — even if it's somebody else's. Further, there is always a danger that so-called protective civil defence leads to the sort of complacency that allows individuals and communities to abdicate responsibility for maintaining world peace and world equality. In this sense, until the world is safe for all humankind we have no right to dig ourselves holes in the ground to retreat into, and when it is eventually safe we shall have no need to.

Ronald Higgins: A measure of protective civil defence can make somewhat more sense for a non-nuclear than a nuclear power. For a start it cannot then be seen as provocative, as a part-preparation for making a first pre-emptive nuclear strike. I cannot follow the usual line than civil defence would be totally useless, especially for a non-nuclear power, but I confess to an instinctive resistance to the despair such preparations would seem to involve.

Mary Kaldor: No, I don't see a role for protective civil defence in a nuclear-free Britain. I used to think that maybe there would be a role — like in Switzerland and Sweden (and that's partly related to my argument about NATO), but I discover that the Swiss and the Swedes are actually very sceptical about their own civil defence programmes.

Stephen Maxwell: The objection to the adoption of civil defence measures by a nuclear power is that they may be seen as part of a war strategy by an adversary. That objection does not apply to a non-nuclear and neutral country. Indeed the provision by such a country of civil defence against nuclear attack will strengthen the credibility of its commitment to resist invasion even by a nuclear power.

Joan Maynard: There would be a role in a nuclear-free Britain. It's a scandal how the present government tries to mislead, though I don't think in fact that they do mislead many people. The majority of people don't believe they can survive a nuclear war, and that's a good thing.

Jonathan Moore: In the context of a militia/mobile force system as outlined earlier, protective civil defence would be an absolutely essential part of a national defence based on deterrence.

The 'unarmed' people will have to be trained and instructed in basic techniques of protection from conventional and nuclear munitions and the general dislocation of life which would occur if an act of aggression was committed against the nation. Some form of counter-measures to chemical weapon attack would be necessary as the possibility of an aggressor using such weapons, particularly for terror purposes, cannot be ruled out, although these could only be of a limited nature. If as envisaged the population is to remain even if overrun, and carry out both 'non-violent' and armed resistance, then training in how to cooperate with and support guerrilla operations, hide weapons, food distribution, dealing with casualties, is essential. A conventional or nuclear attack would require massive medical pre-training of the population; propaganda amongst enemy troops, and preparation generally to maintain resistance behind enemy lines, is concomitant with more passive civil defence measures. Indeed such measures are a basic psychological preparation of the population in the tasks they will have to carry out in resisting an aggressor.

Guerrilla and mobile forces would need the conditions of a 'big country' for successful operations. Due to the geographical nature of Britain's terrain, etc. this could only be obtained by forcing the aggressor to deploy his forces as widely as possible, by continued threats to flanks, rear and front. The result would be combat carried into the urban conurbations, and as Budapest in 1956 and Beirut in 1982 show, heavy fighting with modern weapons amongst an unprepared and unprotected population produces huge civilian casualties.

A shelter-building programme for all public buildings and new housing will be essential. And basic service installations would need some form of protection against damage. The shelters would protect against fall-out from nuclear weapons used by powers outside Britain, and give some form of defence against nuclear blackmail by an outside power. Such a building programme would provide a useful economic stimulant. A programme would be necessary in a militia system, as a large-scale evacuation from even a few cities would be impossible, and such movements would compromise the whole defence system, and its deterrent effect.

Through efficient civil defence organisations, fire, ambulance, medical, police and specialist heavy rescue and anti-chemical task forces would be integrated into the militia system; and particularly with air defence measures. Many personnel to man such services could be recruited from the militia, though basic techniques could be taught at schools, etc.

Such a civil defence system is imperative to 'bring in the nation' to protect the unarmed people and enable the smooth functioning of military operations with as little danger to the same. Most importantly, such measures will contribute to the deterrent power of the system by boosting the morale and commitment of the unarmed people and the militia, increasing their own general feeling of security and confidence in the system, if operations directly or indirectly reach them. Such reasons increase the will of the population to resist; such will is the underpinning of the whole deterrent.

Chris Savory: What would this civil defence be for? If the superpowers have their nuclear weapons, we would still probably be targeted in a nuclear war, as they would not want to leave us to take control in a post-nuclear-war world. Even if this were not true, a system like the Swiss one, designed to protect people from fallout and radiation from a war elsewhere, would be enormously expensive and would take many years to build. The possibilities of civil defence against 'conventional' attack need to be investigated thoroughly.

David Selbourne: I consider 'protective civil defence', *however radically imperfect*, to be both politically essential and a moral imperative; whether Britain disarms or not; and as long as there are nuclear weapons either in existence anywhere in the world, or capable of being manufactured — which is to say permanently, or until a terminal nuclear exchange.

David Taylor: No nuclear war is survivable and no one should be deluded into thinking that it is. Civil defence, however, does not only cover protection against nuclear war. As civilians we have a responsibility to look to our own defence and to that of our communities. Civil defence can be seen as social defence, protection against natural disasters and exploitation as well as invasion. That eventuality is, however, becoming less likely in the modern world. The real threat comes not from without, but from within our own territories, from the ruthless politics of planetary domination in which our environment is used as the tool by which people are exploited. Ultimately the best civil defence is the introduction of a nuclear-free and decentralised system of government.

Dafydd Elis Thomas: Yes, but such protective civil defence should be part of an active voluntary

community action programme which would be available
in all kinds of non-state-induced emergencies.

13   Should women play an equal role in the armed forces at all levels?

Frank Allaun: Whilst believing in equality for women, to suggest that women should play an equal role in the armed forces at all levels is revolting. Military service is in most cases obnoxious for anyone. To suggest that women, who give birth to babies, should take part in preparations for and the carrying out of slaughter of other men, women and children is nauseating. It is flouting the best concepts of civilisation. Florence Nightingale, yes. But the idea of women sticking bayonets into people's stomachs — no!

It can be argued that if it is wrong for women it is equally wrong for men. That argument is correct. Which means that to prepare forces for a nuclear war between America and Russia is unworthy of both sexes.

Pat Arrowsmith: As I don't believe in the armed forces at all, I would think No! I mean, I think women should play an equal role in everything with men, but not believing in the armed forces, I really can't have much sympathy with that.

Meg Beresford: No.

April Carter: This is tricky. There is a case that women should have the right to enter the armed forces if they wish; and I think there is something in the argument that full citizenship implies some obligation to defend one's society. But I do also believe that if women achieve full equality they should use it to change society and to strengthen non-violent values. Going into the armed forces is an extreme example of claiming the right to act like men, rather than challenging male aggressiveness. So I would oppose compulsory military training for women, but probably support the right of individual women to enter the forces, if they choose to do so, on equal terms.

Stuart Christie: If we wish to build a truly democratic defence force then we have to break all the moulds which have limited and restricted us in the past. Every single member of the community — old, young, disabled, male, female, gay, black, white, yellow, etc. — has something they can contribute to such a defence force.

Lisa Foley: Women, like men, should have the right to choose whether or not to join the armed forces. They should be welcomed at any level, but of course hierarchy in the armed forces must be reduced to a minimum. (The goal could be to limit it to three or four broad strata.)

Certain feminists would put forth the argument that women are by nature pacifist and female conditioning to be nurturing and mother-like is actually laudable and should be upheld. Therefore, they would argue, women should have nothing to do with war and non-pacifist forms of resistance.

The flaw with this theory is that it can be used as yet another means of restricting women's role in society. Maybe not all women wish to be nurturing. Maybe some are born fighters.

Robert Fyson: Yes, if they want to. Equal opportunity for women, but no obligation to maintain numerical balance at all levels if recruits were not forthcoming.

Carole Harwood: Women should take a leading role in the systematic dismantling of the whole militarist machine, including the abolition of the armed forces.

Ronald Higgins: This question is more complex than it looks. People of equal capacity for specific tasks should not be barred for arbitrary reasons, e.g. sex. At the other extreme a compulsorily equal sex-quota for the SAS or Paras, or for any other military role, would be ridiculous. Moreover women would in general (note, in general) make reluctant and therefore lousy soldiers, certainly at the sharp end. For this I thank God. And women.

Incidentally my wife's answer to the question was 'only at the top levels!'

Mary Kaldor: No. Absolutely not. I think it's a very good thing women haven't been in the armed forces. The last thing we want to do is to turn women into pretend men. It's the other way round; we want men to accept feminine values. That's my view of feminism.

Joan Maynard: I've never thought about that. I imagine that physically they might not be able to. I wouldn't have thought women would be very keen. I'm not keen on men taking part in the armed forces either.

Chris Savory: Given the traditional links between men and militarism, and the belief that we need to work towards a non-violent defence, women should take at least an equal, and preferably a leading role in all future defence strategies.

David Selbourne: Yes.

John Shiers: Women, of course, must have absolute equality with men in every sphere of social life. There can be no justification for discrimination between women and men, in the armed forces or anywhere else. It is not surprising, however, that existing armed forces throughout the world have excluded women, placed them in subordinate positions or used them to fight when things were really desperate only to send them back to the domestic sphere when pressure slackens off. For so much of military ideology, imagery and fantasy, regardless of the political forces it is representing, is based on male bonding. Men assert the essence of their socially constructed selves through being warriors defending 'their' tribe, 'their' nation, 'their' women and children. But the apparent 'essence' of masculinity is not, in reality, a biological imperative. It is a social role which men learn to play, which has functioned to hold together oppressive ruling classes in power and to subordinate women throughout most, if not all, of human history. The 'masculine' man needs a 'feminine' woman. He needs warmth and tenderness as well as hardness and violence to give his life some purpose. So women have been made to service men's needs, in a feminine role which has been defined in opposition to the masculine (taking account of cultural and historically formed conceptions of what is 'masculine' and 'feminine').

Without the liberation of women and men from the restrictive gender roles we are all forced from birth into occupying, there can be no movement towards a truly equal society. The essence of masculinity is hierarchical, competitive, uncaring and unequal. So it is not a matter of women in the armed forces learning to become like men. Rather it is the opposite. Until men are encouraged to get in touch in themselves with the qualities now considered to be 'womanly' or 'feminine', the new consciousness for non-hierarchical collective forms of organisation simply will not be present, in the armed forces or anywhere else. Part of this must involve both women and men ceasing to repress and deny the potential in all of us to love, and relate sexually, to our own sex. Ending the enforcement of heterosexuality, in girls and boys and in society as a whole, is an important part of moving away from rigid gender roles. It is one which the left, as a whole, has yet to face up to.

Men, as a sex, are going to find all this very difficult. But at least we can stop putting blocks in women's way which prevent them from having the confidence to act in the world. I actually think that the kind of movement towards socialism which I am writing about is highly unlikely to be led by men. The women at Greenham Common have become the spearhead of the new CND in this country, not by doing things in the way of men but by organising collectively as women. So I suspect a new generation of women leaders will emerge who will undermine male power by their effectiveness in creating changes without being leaders in the way that men, whether of the left or the right, have been.

David Taylor: Whilst supporting equal status for women and men in everything, it would be a mistake if we allowed that to cloud this issue. Armies are a profound expression of the patriachy, they are dominated by men because the violence, glory and hierarchies involved have epitomised masculine values for hundreds of years. I cannot imagine most women wanting to play an equal part with men in the armed forces. On the other hand, once a fully democratised and community-based social defence system has been established and is training people in non-violent techniques, I should expect and hope for at least equal participation.

Dafydd Elis Thomas: Yes of course, combatting the macho culture through gender equality would be a direct contribution to the reduction of militarism.

14 Britain is unusual in not having conscription, with responsibility for defence left completely to 'the professionals'. Senior officers, moreover, vigorously oppose the reintroduction of National Service. One reason is clearly that a reluctant army is more troublesome than a willing one. Another may be that conscription would result in the influx of political ideas that at present have little currency in the services, as well as in the wide dissemination of a familiarity with weapons and tactics. Would you support universal military training (or alternatively training in non-violent resistance) if the context were sufficiently democratic? What would this condition mean in practice?

Frank Allaun: In 1957, when conscription was ended, I very well remember the attitude of the War Minister, Brigadier Head. Reflecting the views of the chiefs of the armed forces, he wanted conscription ended for several reasons. The 200,000 national servicemen mainly regarded it as a complete waste of time. They were only anxious to get out quickly, and therefore had a disruptive influence on the regulars. With increasing sophistication of the armed forces and their weaponry, even a two-year course was not sufficient to train them adequately.

I would be completely opposed to compulsory military training, however democratic the context. Service in the forces would probably give many of those concerned a liking for militarism, and induce them towards justifying it in the future when they left the forces.

Training in non-violent resistance is different, but I am not convinced that it could or would be effective. Greater political debate and information, to counter the daily influence of the media, would probably do more to encourage non-violent resistance to a repressive regime than any amount of training. Tam Dalyell MP and other opponents of the Falklands war did more to destroy false patriotism and the macho image than courses in non-violent resistance.

Pat Arrowsmith: Ironically, I can see that if we had conscription — thinking back to the South-East Asia war — it could lead to so much dissidence that it could, perversely, further our objectives. Having said that, as a pacifist I plainly can't support the idea of conscription into the armed forces. But as a pacifist who believes in non-military types of civilian resistance, I would favour a government that tried to foster this. In fact, perhaps, not being an anarchist, I might support the idea of some compulsory mobilisation into non-violent resistance defence activities. I must admit I haven't really thought through this, but it would be such an incredible step were a government to have a non-violent defence policy that were it to insist that people took part in it, it would be such a minor form of compulsion compared to what was going on that it might be acceptable — anyway as I see it at the moment.

Meg Beresford: Training in non-violent resistance, but not universal military training.

April Carter: I have partly covered this question in the answers above. I would not advocate conscription in Britain — I'm not convinced by the political arguments for it and in most circumstances the military arguments for it in a British context are weak. It does also seem a backward step to reintroduce conscription, if the long term goal is to cut armed forces to a minimal police role and to strengthen non-violent values internally and internationally. In certain circumstances — if a non-nuclear Britain opted (with strong popular support) for territorial defence by local militias — I would not actively oppose some form of military training for men, provided there was generous provision for conscientious objection. I would much prefer a national policy of non-violent resistance.

In principle I suppose I would support universal training in non-violent resistance, but in practice I don't believe in formal 'training' in the abstract. There is a case for training for specific demonstrations or actions, but the 'training' for non-violent resistance in general is I think simply political experience, and experience of strikes, boycotts, civil disobedience, etc.

Stuart Christie: I would only support universal military training — or training in non-violent resistance — if I were convinced the context was sufficiently democratic and it was organised on a purely voluntary basis with emphasis on the workplace as the basic militia-training unit. Bonds are strongest there and mutual knowledge deepest. The other headache, of course, would be how to neutralise or minimise the effect of neo-fascist and anti-democratic elements who may try to infiltrate in order to control the defence force at platoon level. Properly structured, however, I don't think they would present much of a danger and contact with a wider circle of people would, I'm sure, have a positive effect on all but the more obsessive and hardened of them.

Lisa Foley: Britain for the time being is not sufficiently endangered to justify universal conscription. For this reason conscription would be unnecessary, not to mention unpopular. Conscription would also be undesirable from the point of view of politicising the armed forces. While socialists would benefit from military training and technique, fascists would too. Familiarity with guns would be useless to the Left unless it was armed. And if the Left managed to legalise gun possession, who else but the law-and-order proponents would go out their way to acquire guns?

Because the Right indisputably holds the reins of power within the military, it would take most — if not all — the energies of the Left to enter and transform the armed forces from within. It has proved hard enough trying to democratise the Labour party, let alone the Army, Navy and Air Force!

Robert Fyson: I don't believe universal military training is necessary, or altogether desirable (see my answer to Question 5). I believe the main reason why senior officers oppose national service is not either of those suggested, but simply because compulsory recruits cost a lot to train and are then only of limited use for a limited period, therefore very expensive. I don't object to a small professional army, as long as it is kept firmly under democratic control.

Carole Harwood: Chatting generally about the democratisation of the army by the introduction of national sevice, I was (sharply!) reminded by my eldest son that what I was talking about was the militarisation of the civilian population and presumably the young, unemployable and 'difficult' section of the population at that. Chastened I began again — this time with realities rather than abstractions.

An examination of 'people's armies' from the 1790s onwards does not suggest that such armies necessarily behave in either a democratic or moral fashion, and the activities of Israel's army in Lebanon brings this scepticism depressingly up to date. I think it unlikely that people can be armed physically without acquiring an armed mentality. I would not wish to see this vicious circle perpetuated in any way.

Regarding training in non-violent resistance — I think it would be essential to any new order and a new order is essential. As for needing the context to be 'sufficiently democratic' I would imagine that the very nature of such training, subversive as it is of traditional authority, would in face *create* a libertarian climate conducive to new ways of thinking, new ways of acting and new ways of living.

Ronald Higgins: This too is a good and difficult question. Most British (but not foreign) professionals say the training burden and hence cost makes conscription impracticable as a basis for modern, high-tech armed forces. These objections are plainly less powerful in relation to creating reserves of less specialised part-time territorials for a strategy of conventional defence in depth. A half-way house of recruiting voluntary territorials in substantial numbers has much to be said for it especially as continuing endemic unemployment would reduce the net effective cost of the policy.

Mary Kaldor: On the one hand I can see very clearly the case for conscription — the political case. On the other hand, I really do believe it would be a militarisation of British society which I would be opposed to.

Stephen Maxwell: The policy of armed neutrality outlined above requires the whole adult population to be considered as part of the nation's defence force. Every active adult would be trained in either violent or non-violent techniques of resistance. Adults would be expected to serve a period of full-time military training to be followed by regular 'refresher' periods. Conscientious objectors to military service would be required to undergo training in non-violent resistance as part of full-time community service of the same duration as the military service.

Joan Maynard: If we have to have an army, I would prefer a conscript army, as it's nearer to the people. Non-violent resistance is absolutely tremendous; look at what Gandhi achieved. But I don't think we have arrived at the stage where we can carry the majority of people with us on this.

Chris Savory: A military, non-provocative 'defence' strategy would rely on advanced technology. Therefore it would certainly not require conscripted armed services or universal military training. Rather, it would need very highly trained, small, mobile and flexible forces. An organised non-violent defence (or social defence), by its very definition, would mean universal training in non-violent resistance. This mobilisation of virtually the entire population is essential if we want to prevent a return of militarism, which could easily happen if we left our 'defence' to an elite group. It would also mean a high degree of cooperation amongst people, and it would greatly empower people as they took on such an important responsibility for their own lives.

David Selbourne: I would support universal military training, whether the context were 'sufficiently democratic' or not — indeed my assumption is that it would not be — for the political reasons already given.

David Taylor: I cannot support any form of conscription, no matter how democratic and even if there was provision for non-violence training. It is simply a matter of principle: people must be able to choose. Locally organised civilian defence training in non-violent resistance should be promoted but not obligatory.

Dafydd Elis Thomas: There is in my view no argument for universal military training. However there is an argument for the opportunity for far more local participation in 'defensive' activities on the ROC model with civilian participation in locally based militia groups which, along the lines of the existing Territorial Army, might conceivably replace a massive professional standing army for armed service on behalf of UNO.

15 Do you see any scope for defence cooperation between a nuclear-free Britain and any other country or countries? What might this involve?

Frank Allaun: There is tremendous scope for defence cooperation between a nuclear-free Britain and other countries. I have attended meetings in Europe along with leaders of the Labour parties from Norway, Denmark, Holland, Belgium and West Germany. They were agreed to do everything possible to refuse cruise missiles in their countries. If they succeed — as I believe they will — this could extend to the complete removal of all nuclear weapons and bases. These governments should aim at non-aggression treaties and détente between East and West.

Pat Arrowsmith: As a pacifist, I can't. I believe in non-violent resistance; it doesn't involve alliances with other countries. Short of that, even though I'm a pacifist I'd see a policy that relied on a conventional army as preferable to what's going on now, and if this involved alliances with other countries that would be somewhat better than the present situation. But I think the moment you start talking about alliances with other countries, involving armies and navies and air forces, this is just a step towards saying, right, we'll use better and better weapons — then before you know where you are you're back into nuclear weapons strategy.

April Carter: There is obviously scope for military cooperation in a nuclear-free NATO or a non-nuclear European defence body. But there could also be scope for cooperation in West European planning for guerrilla warfare or non-violent resistance, either in terms of coordinating resistance or if countries not occupied offered various kinds of practical hope and provided some kind of base for resistance in an occupied country.

Stuart Christie: Most definitely. The more allies or friends you can call on, the more effective your defence will be. However, defence agreements would not be between nation states as such, but rather based on mutual solidarity pacts between genuinely democratic and representative institutions in each country or region. Imagine what a difference a full-blooded task force such as that sent to the Falklands would have had on Franco — to say nothing of Hitler. Obviously the decision to intervene militarily in another country's internal affairs is not one to be taken lightly, but mutual solidarity pacts between representative democracies will be essential if we are to defend ourselves successfully against the forces of reaction.

Lisa Foley: Defence cooperation need not necessarily be military. In case of enemy sanctions or trade embargoes, economic relations could become essential. There is also the possibility of communication links of various sorts between nuclear-free, non-aligned countries (e.g. expensive equipment like satellites) which could assess trends in military escalation worldwide.

On the whole it would probably be wise to steer away from military entanglements with other countries. Once military ties have been built up, it is difficult to dissolve them when no longer needed. And military cooperation could well breed military escalation if it is seen by others as a threat to their national security.

Robert Fyson: Yes, especially the other nations of Western Europe, in non-nuclear, non-CBW, defence planning.

Carole Harwood: I see enormous scope for cooperation between all countries in the unarmed 'defence' of our planet. In reality this would mean the global metropolis combining with the Third World to abolish hunger, poverty and exploitation. It would be a combination of equals subject to a present geographical and historical inequality not beyond the limits of human ingenuity and ability to regulate and ultimately abolish.

Ronald Higgins: Certainly, but as I have said, I don't think we can be 'nuclear-free' in any complete sense and I favour remaining an active member of NATO. Eventually Western Europe could probably be defended almost entirely by conventional forces. Indeed the EEC alone is *rich* enough already to do so (richer by far than the entire Warsaw Pact). All we lack is the political and popular will to do it. (It follows incidentally that NATO's present dependence on the first use of battlefield nuclear weapons is not only silly but a moral scandal.)

This long-term strategy however depends on the Soviet Union not being able convincingly to threaten Western Europe with nuclear attack. And the only presently foreseeable safeguard against this would remain the minimal US strategic nuclear deterrent. This is not moral hypocrisy so long as one argues on grounds of pragmatic good sense not absolute moral principle.

Mary Kaldor: No, I don't see any role for defence cooperation between a nuclear-free Britain and any other countries. I'm very much opposed to that. There's been a lot of discussion on the Left that maybe we should support a West European defensive alliance. I think that's a really terrible idea. I think it would lead to domination by France and Germany in a sinister West European bloc that might be worse than NATO. We've got to move away from the whole idea of military blocs. We don't need to have a defensive alliance. I think one of the reasons people have thought in these terms is that they somehow assume there's a parallel between thinking about defence and thinking about politics. And that's quite wrong. Defence is completely different. That's how people got to the whole idea of citizens' armies being socialist. They're not socialist. Because it's not socialist to depend on physical coercion. It may be socialist to have citizens' bureaucracies but that doesn't mean it's socialist to have citizens' armies. I think that the Left haven't thought enough about the forms of coercion in society. In a sense what capitalism achieved over feudalism and slavery was getting away from individual physical coercion — only having social physical coercion. And our next task, in my view, is that we have to get away from social physical coercion.

Stephen Maxwell: Britain could be nuclear-free and still be a member of NATO, as are Norway and Denmark. A *neutral* Britain would be severely limited in the amount of defence cooperation she could seek with other countries. No doubt British military representatives would have 'exchanges of views' with NATO representatives and probably, for the sake of form, with representatives from the Warsaw Pact countries. There would be scope for cooperation in arms development with other neutral countries such as Sweden and Switzerland.

Joan Maynard: Yes, with other nuclear-free countries. Unilateral nuclear disarmament by Britain could spread the example through Europe. Europe will be the trying-out place for nuclear weapons, if they are ever used, not America or the Soviet Union.

Chris Savory: If Britain adopts a policy of non-violent defence, then presumably by then some other countries would have too. Reciprocal agreements could be made for non-violent intervention into conflicts concerning one or more of these countries. If we reach this stage, I think the most effective form of transnational cooperation would be the creation of non-violent international peace-keeping forces.

In the short term, if Britain was to opt for a military but non-nuclear 'defence' strategy, then a common defence with other European countries would make sense if we were under threat from a superpower.

David Selbourne: The nature of future political relations between nations — whether for purposes of collective defence, trade or aggression — will not be essentially determined by whether they are, or are not, armed with nuclear weapons. Instead, they will be determined as they are now, by the nature of their histories, rivalries, politico-economic systems and ruling classes, and by the forms of dependency, domination and competition which link or separate them. The same applies to Britain.

Therefore, substantially different forms of cooperation from those which exist at present, whether for defence or any other matter, cannot be independently prescribed for.

David Taylor: As one of our principal objectives must be the break-up of the superpower blocs, we must be careful not to create new blocs with which to play the same old game. There is however an advantage to be gained in linking up with other positive, non-aligned countries, especially within Europe. So, I support the extension of the non-aligned movement with greater emphasis on neutralism and the establishment within Europe of a loose alliance of countries on both sides of the Iron Curtain.

16 **Do you see a peace-keeping role for the United Nations, and should Britain be prepared to play a part in a UN peace-keeping force?**

Frank Allaun: There is a big peace-keeping role for the UN. Unfortunately it can only operate at present where small nations are concerned. I see little hope at the moment, in its present development, of the UN keeping the big nations apart. Britain should be prepared to play a vigorous part in the UN peace-keeping force, instead of flouting UN decisions or proposals as it did during the Falklands war. The small remaining parts of the British empire such as Belize, Gibraltar, Hong Kong and the Falklands should come under UN protection, which I believe is immediately practicable. British and other lives should not be lost in trying to defend them.

Pat Arrowsmith: Years ago, just after World War II, I was in the world government movement, involved with many people who felt that only if we had a federally united world were we going to stave off World War III. This was going to involve a world army in effect, though not a nuclear-armed army. It's a question that is very difficult for a pacifist to answer. There are many things short of the ideal. I would think that the ideal would be for people who were being encroached on or invaded by other people to adopt non-violent resistance as their defence against the invaders. But failing that, if some kind of non-military UN peaceful blue line can achieve its purpose and keep the peace, then that's a good thing. I think the problem is that the UN is still very much at the beck and call of the major powers, and it's not in any sense a united world that we're in. But were we to have a united world, with a kind of world police force, then we'd be slap bang up against a highly centralised set-up, with all the potential for, perhaps, having a nuclear armed police force. I haven't got a neat answer to this. In the world as it is at the moment I think effective UN policing is often the best option in certain situations — or better than what might otherwise happen. I mean, take the

South Atlantic. Some position by the UN would have been infinitely better than that absurd and neo-colonialist war we were fighting there. But it's plainly not ideal. It hasn't worked in the Middle East — or only now and again and partially.

April Carter: Yes, the peace-keeping role of the UN is very important, despite its limitations. There is a case for assigning units of armed forces permanently to the UN, so it has forces to draw on in an emergency; certainly Britain should earmark units for UN peace-keeping and explore special training for such units.

Stuart Christie: Well, since it is governments that cause wars in the first place, I don't see any reason for supposing that a committee of governments would be any better than a thieves' kitchen.

Robert Fyson: Yes, to both parts of the question.

Carole Harwood: This is a curiously seductive question until you realise it's asking the same question about the necessity for a standing army. In the case of a UN force you have a highly centralised and presumably armed organisation of soldiers committed to the *'imposition'* of an external solution — see the tragic history of the Congo.
  Instead let's have a global, decentralised, peace-making force armed to the teeth with medical, educational and social skills, trained in all methods of non-violent direct action, completely mobile and completely responsible both to itself and to every section of the global community.

Ronald Higgins: The United Nations already has a peace-keeping role, rightly and necessarily. This should be extended as far as possible. It is however crucial that we recognise that the UN has no effective power to act when the great powers (or therefore their important rival clients) are in conflict. And these conflicts are of course at the heart of the global security problem. We must therefore aim at new arrangements. These will I think need to grow organically out of mutual confidence-building measures reached between the superpowers. The UN as such is only a collection of sovereign powers. It has virtually no power itself beyond that of gradual persuasion. It cannot impose its will. In effect it does not have a will. The UN's potential role in peace-making as well as peace-keeping could nevertheless be substantially enhanced not least in areas of research and contingency planning. Ideas can be as potent as arms. A permanent UN military plus disaster-relief force may gradually produce greater international confidence in the idea of common action.

Britain should plainly contribute substantially in all these fields.

Mary Kaldor: Yes, I do see a peace-keeping role for the UN, and I think we should be prepared to play a part in that.

Joan Maynard: Yes, I wish we could make the UN more effective. But we can only do this when we give up some sovereignty

Stephen Maxwell: Yes and yes.

Ann Pettit: I see no reason why we shouldn't use the United Nations, great lumbering clumsy thing that it has become, to far greater effect. Modern technology, in the hands of the controlling elites of the rich countries, has produced world-wide pollution, world-wide fallout, world-wide recession and a world-wide threat of extinction. Not surprisingly, the response on the part of intelligent people the world over is to 'think globally'. These 'global thoughts' must become translated into ideas on how to outlaw war — how to create _real_ law 'n' order in the world, not by state-organised terrorism, but by international cooperation.

The idea of 'deterrence' is that it is not worthwhile to go to war. We don't necessarily have to throw out this idea. We could change its basis. The economies of France and Germany, for instance, are now so intertwined that war would be economically ludicrous for both parties. Interdependence always reduces the likelihood of conflict. The United Nations 'peace-keeping' force could become a great deal more real — nations could demand that conflicts be solved by discussion, by international law.

This is where women come in — we've always had to use communication, not simple violence, to solve problems, and we've become skilled at it.

Chris Savory: Militarism is intrinsically linked to the concept of sovereign nation states. A non-violent social defence would be based on more decentralised, self-reliant societies. Equally important would be the role of international organisations. The United Nations does seem to have the potential of playing an effective peace-keeping role if enough of the member countries back it with actions as well as words. Britain should play a part in a UN peace-keeping force, a force that should use non-violent techniques of conflict resolution. The demilitari-sation of the world will be a long and hard process, and it will be impossible without many people committing themselves to a strong and positive internationalism.

David Selbourne: The nuclear Sword of Damocles which is suspended over the world can now never be cut down. Even in the best foreseeable case — in which a growingly numerous comity of nuclear disarming nations was making over a large proportion of its non-nuclear forces and/or nuclear weapons to the United Nations, whether for conventional peace-keeping or to provide a nuclear-armed supranational sanction against fractious nations—humanity cannot now be permanent-ly| secured from the risks of nuclear warfare and nuclear knowledge.

Nevertheless, *any* extension of the peace-keeping role of the UN, and of Britain's participation in it, must be considered a step forward.

John Shiers: The United Nations is no more neutral than any other international organisation in the context of world domination by the Western capitalist nations and the Soviet Union. It is potentially, however, an important link between those Western nations that intend to embark on a different course from the one they are currently pursuing and the poor nations of the world.

I do see a role for the United Nations in certain peace-keeping activities and think that England, Wales and Scotland should play a full part in these if they are genuinely to extend or defend the rights of oppressed people as opposed to restoring an oppressive ruling class in power. I also think that the opposition to male-oriented militaristic values, which should characterise the approach of a socialist armed force, should be taken into all our work with other armed forces committed to a just and equal world order.

David Taylor: In June 1945 when the Charter of the United Nations was signed, its purposes were defined as:

1) To maintain international peace and security, and to that end: to take effective collective measures for the prevention and removal of threats to peace, and for the suppression of acts of aggression or other breaches of the peace, and to bring about by peaceful means, and in conformity with the principles of justice and international law, adjustment or settlement of international disputes or situations which might lead to a breach of the peace;

2) To develop friendly relations among nations based on respect for the principle of equal rights and self-determination of peoples, and to take other appropriate measures to strengthen universal peace;

3) To achieve international cooperation in solving

international problems of an economic, social, cultural or humanitarian character, and in promoting and encouraging respect for human rights and for fundamental freedom for all without distinction as to race, sex, language, or religion; and

4) To be a centre for harmonising the actions of nations in the attainment of these common ends.

The United Nations has a powerful and central destiny in the evolution of a peaceful world. Its potential will only be achieved when nations are prepared to trust it and sacrifice more of their sovereignty to it. With sufficient support it could play a much stronger role in resolving territorial disputes — physically, financially and diplomatically. Britain's attitude towards the United Nations is disgraceful; we have to be prepared to commit far more resources, both to the peace-keeping force and to all the other UN agencies.

Dafydd Elis Thomas: Yes, but the basis of defence cooperation should be organised primarily through the international agency of the UN. Such international commitment should have priority over bilateral alliances.

17 Any other comments?

Frank Allaun: To conclude, the peace movement should continue along its present lines, where it is achieving unprecedented and astonishing successes. Our main object should be to prevent an East-West war and to explain that we have to live with the Russians or die with them.

Pat Arrowsmith: The world is such an incredibly difficult place, given that there are weapons that could very likely destroy all human life — or most of it; so really one does have to look for totally other ways of achieving one's ideals — in my case, socialism and humanitarian values. I expect other people would claim they were supporting humanitarian values, even though I mightn't think that they were. But you can't claim to be backing such values with a weapon which is a total contradiction of them. So people really have to look for quite other means of doing so — we've got to find another way.

Robert Fyson: In the short time available to us in order to avert nuclear holocaust, we cannot hope to radically transform human patterns of behaviour, or alter the whole basis on which the internal organisation of nation states, and their relations with each other, are organised. The only chance of success for any alternative defence policy being adopted at present is if it can be shown to be practicable and realistic, within the parameters of 'common sense' as currently understood by most people outside the peace movement. Too much vague utopianism is a disservice to our cause, but the substitution of conventional for nuclear defence policies could be a real step towards survival, and the ultimate long-term goal of a substantially disarmed world.

Carole Harwood: Trying to answer the questionnaire with complete honesty I became increasingly aware of the need to challenge some of the questions' assumptions.

Having done this it is necessary to follow the logic of one's position to its logical conclusion — not always a comfortable practice. It seems to lead to a putting-oneself-outside-of the comforting and familiar politics that have, up till now, provided such pat answers, and replacing all such panaceas with a personal responsibility within a collective and caring context. Perhaps the danger of all previous 'isms' is that they invariably provide a cop-out clause. It will no longer do. The world has shrunk; we are now simply survival clusters of an endangered species faced with two alternatives ... We can huddle together for warmth and share for survival, or retain a prestigious segregation and perish. We have no other choices.

Ronald Higgins: Plenty but there is all too little room! Any predetermined framework of questions, for all its merits, is bound to distort one's position. I shall therefore say that I stand by the views outlined in my tract *Neither Hawk Nor Dove* which outlines what I think the wisest position, that of the 'Owl'.

This is one which sustains a painfully dual recognition of the collective madness implicit in the nuclear arms race but also of the treacherous and immediate, political and military, realities of a volatile world. Mere revulsion is not enough: we have to transpose it into practical policies aimed at reducing the chances of mass indiscriminate slaughter by whatever sorts of wea-ponry.

This means refashioning our basic philosophy (even theology) of security without losing touch with all the various factors that can be easily subtract from international stability. Not only must we take note of Soviet capabilities and (persisting) aims and fears but also of how, say, France or West Germany might react to any large change in British policy. We sometimes need reminding that statecraft is always about getting from here to there, not the design of utopia. Folly too is a sin.

Another aspect of our folly, and one found amongst

hawks and doves alike, is a preoccupation with weapon systems as opposed to political processes. We tend to think disarmament is a greater cause than détente despite the fact that warheads could be cut by 90 per cent and still destroy our species. Arms control negotiations and the rest can of course contribute to détente. But in these too the political, and *personal*, processes are crucial.

Some of us, not least my colleagues in the Dunamis project, based at St James's Church, Piccadilly, would therefore like to see much more attention given to these human factors. Like many others we are trying to relate fundamental moral, spiritual and psychological dimensions to the security debate. We are also searching for the vital elements of a more creative diplomacy. Much recent work in techniques of communication, conciliation and conflict resolution may prove fertile. We have to look not only at the context and content but the very methods and manner of negotiation.

No less important, following twenty years of largely fruitless disarmament negotiation, we are looking at the potential of audacious measures, ways of tipping sideways the frozen kaleidoscope of East-West confrontation, just as President Sadat's landing at Jerusalem transformed Israeli-Egyptian confrontation. We might hope, as he did, that common, 'super-ordinate' goals can be perceived and pursued despite the persistence of real, even bitter, differences.

Ultimately of course the greatest common interest must be survival itself. The nuclear revolution demands that humanity rapidly goes through a profound learning experience. We are all now involved in what could be the species' last chance. This learning experience is not least difficult for ministers and officials submerged by urgent and successive crises.

There may therefore be a special onus on those like us who do not share these daily trials. We ourselves need to learn to listen quietly and speak scrupulously. Violence can be psychic as well as physical. The facile assertion of our own 'principles' (and righteousness) can be cruel as well as silly.

The 'peace movement' has tended so far to neglect two key tasks. The first is to create robust and credible non-nuclear (or less nuclear) defence policies, the prime and welcome aim of this volume. The second is to acquire the undogmatic tone of voice crucial to public persuasiveness and hence to political success.

Most of the expert adherents of current NATO orthodoxies are as dedicated to peace as any of us. To varying degrees the reader, like this writer, may disagree with much of their analysis and conclusions. But only constructive reason not moral obloquy will produce the changes we need. And that applies to both sides.

This in turn may demand of us a certain amount of quiet self-examination, as inward journey that can proceed in tandem with the equally necessary outward journey into the abstract language of politics and defence. Some of us are setting up small informal groups in which to explore these intersecting dimensions together. It is well worth it! We are in for a very long haul.

Joan Maynard: The question of peace and getting rid of nuclear weapons is top priority. We should strive with all our might and main to achieve it. We hold the world in trust, and we have no right to poison it for future generations. If anybody isn't in the peace movement, they ought to join now.

Ann Pettit: So long as arms trades and industries flourish, we shall have wars and a whole war-games machinery both mental and physical. In the end, it is up to all the people of the world who know that the military sector takes from them what is rightly theirs, to demand back their share of the technology, that we make a start at cultivating the arts of peace instead of war. There are a myriad ways of defending oneself against attack once attack has happened; but while swords are made at the expense of ploughshares, the conditions that create insecurity and war will persist.

Chris Savory: It is good that the development of ideas about military and non-military defence strategies for a nuclear-free Britain should continue together. The more different ideas that we have, the more likely we are to come up with something that works. When the disarmament process actually starts, it is very hard to know what will happen, and at what speed. So a variety of options is essential. At the moment I see a non-violent social defence strategy as the logical conclusion of disarmament. Obviously, though, this is going to require an enormous amount of hard work and far-reaching social change. Such a defence strategy will only be viable, I believe, in a decentralised yet internationally orientated society. So a fundamental change of values will be necessary. We will have to eventually rid ourselves of patriarchy, profit/greed-orientated production and nation states as well as militarism, as in fact they all go together. This will probably be a long and painful process. As we struggle towards our ideal society, many steps and stages and compromises will be necessary. Perhaps the first step will be European nuclear disarmament, followed by the implementation of a non-provocative defence policy for Europe, but we must not stop there.

In general, we must concentrate more and more on conflict resolution, rather than continually preparing for and participating in war.

David Taylor: An alternative defence programme needs to consider deeply the root causes of war. Nuclear weapons are not a nasty accident in an otherwise healthy world, but the logical expression of the diseased, violent values which govern our social and governmental institutions. The root causes are economic, cultural and social. Their remedy involves a deep-rooted shift in the guiding values of our society, and the evolution of non-violent techniques for the resolution of human conflict.

Dafydd Elis Thomas: As a former teacher of language and social studies I am most anxious to demystify the language used by politicians, the media and military experts in dealing with 'defence'. This is where the whole development of peace studies could provide for a major shift in public understanding of defence and armed force in the world context. More than anything we need 'ideological disarmament', where we are able to disabuse ourselves of the state-reproduced notions of defence and 'national interest'. It is not possible to separate discussion of 'defence' from discussion of the rest of the economic and social life of states. The present organisation of states and their political structure lead to the kind of defence policies which they deploy. Changes in defence can only be carried through successfully in my view if they are paralleled by changes on the broader economic and social front. Educational and ideological change must occur simultaneously if peace changes are to be maintained. The lessons of the containment of successive peace campaigns in Britain, particularly those opposed to the use of nuclear weapons, is explained by their absorption as single-issue campaigns into what is a very soggy British political culture.

A Third World View of the Peace Movement

Bennie Bunsee: The peace movement which is searing across the European continent is the biggest and most important mass movement of its kind, cutting across class boundaries and parties and being truly a people's movement. The question of preventing a nuclear war has quickly overshadowed every other burning political issue and to a very large extent has become the focal point of the global crisis facing humanity. A new and frightening word has been coined to express the awesome destructive power of nuclear war — exterminism. It is the first time this word has been used to describe human wars, not omitting the genocide committed against black races during the early period of Western colonialism. No one in their right mind will dispute that the total abolition of nuclear weapons is the only sane policy for our world, and all talk about deterrence, 'balance of terror', etc. reveals a mental incapacity to come to terms with reality.

But the meaning of peace must be given a deeper content, eventually encompassing all the issues of human liberation to achieve a qualitative leap into a radically new type of society, free from the disharmonies that now mark every field of human activity. A pacifist approach to the issues of war and peace is disastrously limited, and self-defeating. Of course the peace movement which has mushroomed over the past few years in still in the infancy of its development. Larger questions loom around it and it will not be a viable movement until it addresses itself to these, for the question of peace (and non-violence) is intimately linked to questions of social and human liberation. Its appearance on the European scene coalesces with other pressing and dynamic movements of political liberation. Fed into the peace movement are various political trends, ecological, feminist, etc. Each trend brings with it its particular political outlook. Can a synthetical approach to political and human liberation arise out of the convergence of these various viewpoints at a time when humanity is faced with a global crisis of survival

never known in its history? We are on the threshold of
Armageddon. And it is no more possible for the Third
World to ignore the consequences of a nuclear war,
distant as this might appear to the starving, miserable
millions, than it is for Europe to gawp with passive
sympathy at the plight of the Third World.

Traditional radical socialist politics, as we associate
this with the Communist parties and what is generally
regarded as the Marxist left in Europe, is in a state of
crisis — is it the failure of the traditional approach? —
and the vacuum is being filled by mass movements
centring around single issues of which the peace movement has emerged as the most important and massive. I
believe that these extra-parliamentary movements will
serve as the new starting-points of analysis for political
and human liberation in Europe at a time when the
traditional panaceas of the Left are at a nadir. I do not
believe that the traditional answers relating to class,
state, and war and revolution are in any way irrelevant,
but the old bottles will have to be filled with new wine.
Many holes can be punched into the peace movement,
discrepancies shown and major weaknesses underlined.
But I believe this is not a constructive approach, as the
peace movement is a genuine and authentic movement
touching the hearts and minds of millions deeply
concerned and worried about the future survival of the
world. Humanity has arrived at that conjuncture of
world history when it either has to take a courageous
leap into human liberation and discard the centuries-old
baggage of its thinking, or literally sink into the mire of
barbarism. We cannot take consolation here in the myth
of Sisyphus, of the stone rolling back to its original
position. This time it will drag us all into the abyss. No
nation, country or people is exempt from the peril.

But bear with Third World revolutionaries if they
might in unwary moments approach the question of
nuclear war with cynicism. They have since World War
II seen many of their countries devastated by bombs and
armaments emanating from the rich West no less

destructive and lethal than a nuclear bomb. We have
before us the carpet bombing of Vietnam and
Kampuchea that left vast areas of the countryside not
only uninhabitable but also uncultivatable. And while
nuclear disarmers stomped through the cities of
London, Paris and Washington, only yesterday the
ancient and historical city of Beirut was ruthlessly razed
to the ground, thousands of men, women and children
killed and hundreds of thousands more made homeless.
Despite all the hypocritical sentiments expressed about
Sabra and Chatilla the dismemberment of Lebanon goes
on, colonial-type settlements are forced in the West
Bank and Gaza to make a future Palestinian homeland
unviable. It is the imperialist method of the creation of
facts. You destroy somebody else's home, set up your
own home in its stead and when asked to move you reply
cynically: 'But I live here now, where should I go to?' In
El Salvador about three thousand people are killed
monthly by a fascist military junta armed and backed by
the United States (Britain was the only Western country
which attempted to give a gloss to the recently rigged-up
elections). The list is endless. And if Third World
revolutionaries have not meaningfully participated in
the disarmament debate and might even regard it as a
European pastime, it is because they know and
experience daily the unending process of imperialist
oppression and its relentless violence. Many believe that
while European disarmers rave about disarmament, it is
in their countries that a nuclear war will be fought out.
They see the wars engendered in their countries by the
two superpowers as experimental grounds for weapons
they wish to test for some future greater combat. (It is
encouraging to note that at the last END conference in
Brussels a workshop argued that 'peace movements in
Europe cannot remain Eurocentric and forget struggles
in other parts of the world', and that 'the danger of a
third world war arises essentially from the policies and
rivalry of the superpowers in the world, and the Third
World in particular'.)

It is here that we get to a key question in considering any alternative defence policy for Britain. We first have to answer the question, what is the nature of the British state which eventually presides over all its public and foreign affairs? The simple answer is that Britain is an imperialist state with vast world-wide imperialist interests which form its economic foundations. After all, Britain is involved in a war of repression right at home in Ireland, a national liberation struggle of profound importance for the future of the British state. As a major partner in the NATO alliance and chief ally of the USA, it participates in all its predatory policies. During the Malvinas crisis Britain stationed nuclear submarines off the islands. Nor was this the first time that the threat of nuclear weapons had been used there. It still is.

Another question we have to answer in considering an alternative defence policy is, who threatens the national independence of Britain? 'The Russians': that is the official explanation given us by the ruling classes. Any war that takes place between the Warsaw Pact and the NATO bloc led by the USA will be a war among imperialist predators for another re-division of the world's resources. No victory by either the Russians or the Western imperialists will result in an era of freedom and democracy for humanity. It will leave one group of predators to continue as before. Britain as part of the Western imperialist bloc threatens the national independence of other countries. And while it does not actually send its armies racing across the seas as of yore (except for minor skirmishes like the Malvinas), it fully participates in the neo-colonial domination of the South. Britain has certainly supported every US policy since World War II. Neo-colonialism, the propping up of corrupt, murderous, tyrannical elites in the Third World, is the modern form of imperialist domination; the financial strangulation of the export of capital takes the place of the export of conquering armies. Britain is the second largest contributor to the IMF which tries to regulate the world's finances in the interests of imperialism.

Wars do not just happen. They are the products of human action and thinking. The whole epoch of imperialism from its earliest mercantile phase to the present is littered with wars. The exterminism of a possible nuclear war is the culminating point of this destructive and soul-destroying exploitative system. Wars cannot be separated from the imperialist system. The abolition of wars must mean eventually the total abolition of this system. Violence (big and small) is the coercion exercised by exploiting classes to protect their interests.

War, and particularly a world war that involves two big blocs and draws other countries and nations into the maelstrom, is the culminating point in the aggravation of class antagonisms and social tensions. The march towards a destructive and exterminist nuclear war, in fact, is the result of all the aggravations on a world level of class, social and national tensions, waiting like an over-ripe boil to burst. The halt to nuclear weapons — absolutely necessary as this is — will not result in anything like peace for us. The social tensions of all kinds, which today have reached global proportions and fragment the harmony of human relations, will still be with us driving us in the same direction of a destructive lunacy. The peace movement will have to deepen its meaning of peace to mean not only the abolition of nuclear weapons but also the abolition of those class and social tensions that set nation against nation, that result in civil strife instead of civil liberties within nations, and that create a malaise and sickness which penetrates into the very pores of our individual existences, making so many of us malleable mental cripples. And while non-violence is a necessary corollary of peace and a genuine people's democracy, it must be obvious that its only fertile soil is the elimination of class antagonisms which constitute the breeding ground of every social antagonism in our societies. Peace, non-violence and democracy. In many ways they are inter-related words and terms. But they can only be realised when their real meaning is not subverted to mean war, violence and tyranny, to which bourgeois rhetoric has reduced them in our real world. The elimination of nuclear weapons will not make our social relations less violent; non-violence in the long run is a state of the mind and the heart, conduced by social conditions that bring out the best in human beings and not the worst.

It is in the realm of imperialism and class struggle, and in the revolutionary transformation of society these antagonisms give rise to, that the peace movement will find its real answers; in particular the dialectic between imperialism, the class struggle, and war and revolution, a process well under way in our world which the peace movement will eventually have to relate to if it does not wish to defeat its own ends and lead to disillusionment. We are at the same moment in European history that led to World Wars I and II, and the same forces of barbarism are slowly being unleashed as occurred then.

These issues have been focussed on before by the traditional Left (especially the Communist movement and the Marxist left of all varieties), but that stream in Western European politics has today run out of much steam. Rudolf Bahro argues that the traditional Left view of society is now archaic, and calls for a radical new thinking to address ourselves to the same goals of peace, democracy and socialism. While I do not agree with his thesis of the irrelevance of traditional Marxist-Leninist analysis, I would at least agree that much of the politics of the Left has become stereotyped. What he calls the 'failed socialism' of the socialist countries has duplicated the capitalist type of relations and disillusioned many. Much of the behaviour of the traditional Left is dogmatic and sectarian. (To a large extent this is due to its immaturity.) While the goals and analysis remain the same — it is in fact unresolved problems that result in the same crisis — there is most certainly the need for a fresh approach, especially when the labour movement remains in torpor, confined within reformist and economistic illusions about the nature of capitalism.

Traditionally European thinking has tended to place the imperialist dimension of its history at the periphery. It has only responded to it under pressure and has generally not shown an ability to relate to it integrally. Bahro, however, does precisely this. He opens up the imperialist dimension of Western history and civilisation which has wreaked so much havoc and pillage outside its own perimeters, especially on the Third World, and which today threatens the survival of the human race with a nuclear war. The West, and the peace movement in particular, must realise that it is integrally bound up with the Third World which it has battened onto and oppressed for centuries.

Third World, First World. There is only one world. We are all in this together. Imperialism and class struggle are the links.

Suggested reading

Alternative Defence Commission *Defence Without the Bomb* (Taylor & Francis 1983)

Rudolf Bahro *Socialism and Survival* (Heretic Books 1982)

Frank Barnaby and Egbert Boeker *Defence Without Offence* (Housmans 1982)

Frank Barnaby and Stan Windass 'Defence Without Tears' *Democrat* November 1982

Leonard Beaton *The Reform of Power* (Chatto & Windus 1971)

Board for Social Responsibility of the Church of England *The Church and the Bomb* (Hodder & Stoughton 1982)

Eugene Burdick and Harvey Wheeler *Fail-safe* (Hutchinson 1963)

Ernest Callenbach *Ecotopia* (Pluto 1978)

April Carter, David Hoggett and Adam Roberts *Non-Violent Action: a selected bibliography* (Housmans 1970)

Stuart Christie *Towards a Citizens' Militia* (Cienfuegos 1979)

Brian Easlea *Fathering the Unthinkable* (Pluto 1983)

David Fernbach *The Spiral Path* (Gay Men's Press 1981)

David Fernbach 'Tom Wintringham and Socialist Defence Strategy' *History Workshop Journal 14* autumn 1982

Louis Fischer *The Life of Mahatma Gandhi* (Granada 1982)

Sally Miller Gearheart *The Wanderground* (Persephone 1980)

The Green Pack (4 Bridge House, St Ives, Huntingdon, Cambridgeshire)

A Green View of Peace (Green CND, 14 Alexandra Road, Oxford)

Ronald Higgins *Neither Hawk Nor Dove* (Radical Centre 1982)

Ronald Higgins *The Seventh Enemy* (revised edition Hodder & Stoughton1982)

David Horowitz *From Yalta to Vietnam* (Penguin 1967)

Independent Commission on Disarmament and Security Issues [Palme commission] *Common Security* (Pan 1982)

Independent Commission on International Development Issues [Brandt commission] *North-South: a programme for survival* (Pan 1981)

Coretta Scott King *My Life With Martin Luther King* (Hodder & Stoughton 1970)

Stephen King-Hall *Defence in the Nuclear Age* (Gollancz 1958)

Labour Party Working Party on Defence *Sense About Defence* (Quartet 1977; sequel to be published 1983)

George Lakey *Strategy for a Living Revolution* (Freeman 1973)

Bert 'Yank' Levy *Guerrilla Warfare* (Penguin 1941)

Loompanics Unlimited catalogue (P O Box 264, Mason, MI 48854, USA)

Chris Mullin *A Very British Coup* (Hodder & Stoughton 1982)

NATO Information Service publications (1110 Brussels, Belgium)

Robert Nield *How To Make Up Your Mind About the Bomb* (Deutsch 1981)

Adam Roberts *The Strategy of Civilian Resistance* (Penguin 1969)

Adam Roberts *Nations in Arms* (Chatto & Windus 1976)

Jonathan Schell *The Fate of the Earth* (Pan 1982)

Gene Sharpe *Making the Abolition of War a Realistic Goal* (Housmans 1980)

Gene Sharpe *The Politics of Non-Violent Action* (3 vols; Boston Porter Sargent 1973)

Dan Smith *The Defence of the Realm in the 1980s* (Croom Helm 1980)

Dan Smith *Non-Nuclear Military Options for Britain* (Housmans 1982)

Tom Wintringham *New Ways of War* (Penguin 1940)

Tom Wintringham *People's War* (Penguin 1943)

The contributors

Frank Allaun has been Labour MP for Salford East since 1955. He helped organise the first Aldermaston march and took part for many years in the Easter marches in England and West Germany. He is chairperson of Labour Action for Peace, and of the Labour Party Working Party on Defence. Author of *Questions and Answers About Nuclear Weapons*, *Stop the H-Bomb Race*, etc.

Pat Arrowsmith helped found the Direct Action Committee Against Nuclear War in 1958, and is still very active in CND today. She has stood three times for Parliament on anti-war issues, and been jailed ten times for political offences. Since 1971 she has worked full-time for Amnesty International. She is also a poet, novelist and painter.

Meg Beresford spent her formative years in a community one of whose principles was conscientious objection — hence a third-generation pacifist by conviction as well as nature. She was active in grass-roots community politics before the peace movement, and is now a full-time worker for END, also involved with CND. Her views are personal and neither CND nor END policy.

Bennie Bunsee is an Azanian revolutionary writer and activist, and editor of *Ikwezi* magazine. He has been involved in anti-racist struggles in Britain and led some of the major Asian workers' strikes in the Midlands.

April Carter was secretary of the Direct Action Committee Against Nuclear War 1958-61, and chairperson of CND 1970-71. She now teaches politics at Somerville College, Oxford, and is a member of the Alternative Defence Commission.

Stuart Christie is an anarchist writer and publisher. He was imprisoned in Spain 1964-67 for an attempt on the life of Franco, and in Britain 1971-72 before being acquitted in the 'Angry Brigade' trial. He is the author of *Floodgates of Anarchy*, *The Christie File*, *Towards a Citizens' Militia* and *The Investigative Researcher's Handbook*.

Lisa Foley has worked for the Alternative Defence Commission since it was first brought together in 1980. As a socialist-feminist she is active in the labour movement and women's groups in Bradford.

Robert Fyson teaches history at North Staffordshire Polytechnic. He has been actively involved in CND since 1958, and secretary of the Liberal CND and Peace Group since 1980. He is a member of the CND national executive.

Carole Harwood: 'I have answered the questionnaire as a woman involved with and committed to the politics, mentality and "actions" of the Greenham Common Women's Peace Camp. I don't, however, speak for my sisters, all of whom can, and do, speak for themselves. By training I am a historian at present engaged in trying to ensure that "history" will continue.'

Ronald Higgins served for thirteen years in the British diplomatic service before working for eight years at the *Observer*. Then he wrote *The Seventh Enemy*, on the human factors in the global crisis, made a film about it, and later became a freelance writer and lecturer. Since 1980 he has also been consultant to the Dunamis project for redefining security.

Mary Kaldor is a fellow of the Science Policy Research Unit and the Institute of Development Studies at Sussex University. She is the author of *The Disintegrating West* and *The Baroque Arsenal*, a member of the END coordinating committee and editor of *END Journal*.

Stephen Maxwell is honorary fellow in politics at Edinburgh University and a former vice-chairperson of the Scottish National Party. Between 1966 and 1969 he was engaged in research on nuclear strategy and deterrence theory at the London School of Economics and the International Institute for Strategic Studies. He has recently been active as convenor of the steering committee of the Scottish Socialist Society.

Joan Maynard has been Labour MP for Sheffield, Brightside since October 1974, and was on the National Executive Committee of the Labour party from 1972 to 1982. She comes from a rural background, and is sponsored by the Agricultural and Allied Trades group of the TGWU. She is a vegetarian, and lives in Thirsk, North Yorkshire.

Ann Pettit is a smallholder, and organiser of the Women For Life on Earth peace-march to Greenham Common, 1981. She is a grass-roots activist in the peace movement, and an occasional writer (and even more occasional painter) when she gets time.

Chris Savory is a student at the School of Peace Studies, Bradford University. He is active in CND and the Ecology party, and describes himself as a realistic idealist.

David Selbourne read law at Balliol, and has been tutor in politics at Ruskin College, Oxford since 1965. He is the author of *An Eye to India, Through the Indian Looking-Glass* and *The Making of A Midsummer Night's Dream*. He has published widely as a political journalist and essayist since the mid 1970s.

John Shiers has been a community worker in London and Manchester for the past five years, and active on the radical end of the gay movement since 1971. He is currently involved with the Labour Campaign for Gay Rights, as a shop steward at his workplace, and in campaigning around local issues in Hulme.

Peter Tatchell is a left-wing socialist active in the Labour party. He is strongly committed to peace and disarmament, and the creation of a genuinely defensive and distinctively democratic system of non-nuclear defence. He is the Labour parliamentary candidate for Bermondsey, where he lives.

David Taylor has helped organise many Green gatherings and is a founder member of Green CND. He contributes regularly to *Green Line* magazine and is co-editing a book on the political role of the Green movement.

Dafydd Elis Thomas has been a tutor in Welsh studies at Harlech College and the University College of North Wales, and a part-time broadcaster for BBC Wales and HTV. Since February 1974 he has been Plaid Cymru MP for Merioneth.

Ruth Wallsgrove is active in Women Oppose the Nuclear Threat, and works as a member of the *Spare Rib* collective. She writes here in a personal capacity.

David Widgery is a doctor working in general practice in East London. He was the editor of *The Left in Britain 1956-68*, the sequel to which will be published in 1986. His next book (1983) is *Making Time*, a study of racism and music. He has been a member of the Socialist Workers Party and its various predecessors since 1967.

*

Louis Mackay works as a graphic artist and translator from Scandinavian languages. His political involvements have included anti-racist work, CND and END, and he is on the editorial collective of Heretic Books.

David Fernbach works for Gay Men's Press and Heretic Books, and is also on the Heretic editorial collective. He has taken part in a range of radical movements since the early 1960s, and is author of *The Spiral Path: a gay contribution to human survival*.